ARCHITECTURE FOR TEENS

ARCHITECTURE
FOR TEENS

A Beginner's Book for Aspiring Architects

DR. DANIELLE S. WILLKENS,
Associate AIA, FRSA, LEED AP BD+C

ILLUSTRATIONS BY
CLAIRE ROLLET

callisto
publishing
an imprint of Sourcebooks

Copyright © 2021 by Callisto Publishing LLC
Cover and internal design © 2021 by Callisto Publishing LLC
Illustrations © Claire Rollet, 2021
Author photography courtesy Candace Willkens
Series Designer: Lisa Forde
Interior and Cover Designer: Patricia Fabricant
Art Producer: Tom Hood
Editors: Nadina Persaud and Andrea Leptinsky
Production Manager: Holly Haydash
Production Editor: Melissa Edeburn

Published by Callisto Publishing LLC C/O Sourcebooks LLC
P.O. Box 4410, Naperville, Illinois 60567-4410
(630) 961-3900
callistopublishing.com

Printed in the United States of America
VP 24

For Mom

CONTENTS

INTRODUCTION

HELLO! I am Danielle Willkens, your guide to the exciting world of careers in architecture. I'm an architectural designer and architectural historian, which means I'm interested in the intersection of where we come from and where we are going in the built environment. I use the tools of architectural practice, such as drawing and physical and digital modeling, to document, interpret, and preserve historic sites. I also aspire to bring new life to these sites, so my design work reimagines how we can experience and interact with our world.

Architecture is a wonderfully complex and varied field that integrates technology, physics, artistic expression, material science, and even psychology, and thanks to my work, I've been fortunate to visit famous ancient sites and revolutionary projects across the globe, both in person and virtually.

My love of the field is rooted in my childhood interests: drawing, understanding how things work, and problem-solving. From the time I could pick up a crayon, it was rare to find me without a sketchbook or my building blocks. I was fascinated by new types of digital technologies and by my great-great-uncle, an engineer whose drafting table was filled with tools, sketches, and drawing instruments. His career as a problem-solver and creator helped inspire my dream of assembling projects from my imagination.

I pursued several degrees and started my career as an intern architect at both a small residential firm and a larger corporate one. I became a historic interpreter and researcher at a UNESCO World Heritage Site, a design/build project manager for a floating field station and sustainable classroom, and a field researcher at various historic sites using traditional surveying methods as well as cutting-edge tools such as 3D scanners and drones. Now I am an educator in architectural design and architectural history. I love introducing young students to the world of design and working with both undergraduate and graduate students on research and creative projects that investigate how we can build a sustainable, resilient, and inclusive world—and I am very excited to offer this book to you.

This book will give you the opportunity to learn about a wide array of topics within the study and creation of the built environment. You will be introduced to important movements and designers, and we will delve into the work of several contemporary architects who will share how and what they do as well as what inspires their work. You will come to see that buildings are like onions: To fully understand a piece of architecture, you need to identify all its layers.

Architecture is a multifaceted and ever-evolving field. I hope this book and its explorations will spark your curiosity and creativity, leading to the pursuit of a path in architectural design that you will find inspiring and rewarding.

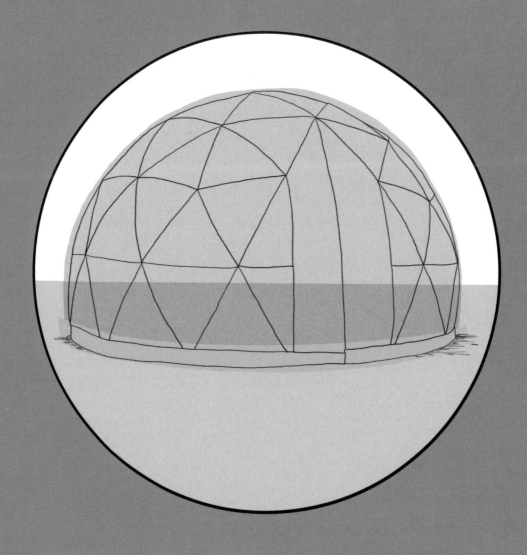

Chapter 1
ARCHITECTURE 101

TO BETTER UNDERSTAND THE BUILT ENVIRONMENT AND BE SUCCESSFUL DESIGNERS, architects need to study the foundations of architecture. For every architect, the past informs the potential of the future. It's important to examine the built work of different cultures, places, and eras as well as the work of specific architects and design firms. By studying the projects of the past alongside contemporary design trends, we can better understand how to create a more inclusive and sustainable world. This chapter explores some key movements and figures within the history of architecture as well as the practice of architecture and the role of the architect.

WHAT IS ARCHITECTURE?

At the most basic level, architecture is shelter. It protects us from the elements and provides comfort within a controlled environment. Architectural historian Sir Nikolaus Pevsner pushed the definition further with an analogy: "A bicycle shed is a building; Lincoln Cathedral is a piece of architecture." But we have to think bigger and broader to truly define architecture.

When we talk about architecture, we are considering both the act of creating an object and the object itself. Architecture is experimental, tackling new building methods, difficult climates, and sites with relentless environmental forces such as earthquakes. Architecture is also an art form. Depending on the design, buildings can be powerful and intimidating or whimsical and playful; they can be peaceful and somber or fun and creative. Architecture is an incredible chameleon because there are so many forms, materials, sites, and creative approaches.

To fully understand architecture, we can remember the essential components of architectural analysis through the acronym **SPEAR:**

STRUCTURE: What are the key structural elements and forces that act on the building, whether natural (wind or seismic zones) or human-made (dead loads from the weight of all the building components or live loads from occupants)?

PROGRAM: How does the building function? Some structures have multiple uses, whereas others belong to a particular typology, such as residence, school, office, or hospital.

ECONOMICS: Buildings are expensive, so who funded and maintains the building and why?

AESTHETICS: What are the essential visual elements of the building? Is it conventional or atypical for a particular time or place?

REGION: Where is the building located and how does the climate, geography, and culture have an impact on the design? Conversely, how does the building shape its site?

We can use architecture as one of the primary ways to study cultures and eras and inform our designs for the future.

HISTORY OF ARCHITECTURE

The world is full of fascinating structures, but learning the stories behind buildings and understanding how to read architecture can make history come alive. In addition to a broad range of knowledge from drawing to technical expertise in construction, architects also need to understand the history of the built environment. They must study not only buildings, but also landscapes such as gardens and parks, elements of infrastructure like bridges and tunnels, and large-scale urban plans.

Across the globe, buildings are responding to different cultural, geographic, and historic associations. Studying buildings allows us to discover the many connections between different eras and architects. For example, wood is a building material used across time and in different locations. Or think of a common building component like a porch, which is an example of how different architects adapted a simple feature to provide shelter from wind and rain while enhancing the overall form and applied decoration of a structure.

Ruins, archaeological sites, and architectural drawings and writings can also be excellent resources for understanding how architecture has evolved. All these elements can help us understand how a project used new building technologies, advanced construction practices, and met the unique needs of both patrons and the general population. There are countless examples of notable architecture around the world.

WHY BE AN ARCHITECT?

If you ask practicing architects why they became interested in their profession, many will tell you they were fascinated with building kits and blocks. Others will say they constantly drew, imagined inventions, and were curious about how mechanical objects and structures worked. Architects create meaningful places to improve the lives of inhabitants and strengthen communities.

On a basic level, architects are responsible for satisfying the fundamental human need for shelter. But architects are responsible for creating so much more than simple buildings. As professionals who blend art and science, architects shape the physical world through their designs. Their work impacts both public and private realms. They explore new materials and fabrication systems that test the limits of technology. They make captivating, distinguished structures that can even evoke emotions. Have you ever encountered a piece of architecture that left you awestruck? Think about a recent vacation or field trip where you visited a piece of architecture. At one point, that building was just an idea, but an architect brought it to life.

Architects are problem-solvers. At the core of the architectural profession is the concept of design thinking. Architects are inventive. They tackle spatial problems by drawing and modeling their ideas. They are tasked with designing structural interventions that slow deterioration from the elements. They are challenged to reinvent abandoned or underused sites. Architecture is a great field if you want to work within the realms of engineering, artistic expression, history, memory, and environmentalism, among others. It's also an ideal enterprise for anyone who wants to protect and interpret the past while imagining how we can build a better future.

Prehistoric (before 3500 BCE): As the earliest societies formed, people created gathering sites to build communities, and three main categories of architecture emerged. With pit constructions, builders excavated the earth to create sunken spaces for dwelling and rituals (Çatalhöyük and Skara Brae, left). Megalithic structures moved and organized large stones into monumental constructions (Newgrange and Stonehenge). Subtractive architecture involved removing material from existing rock formations to create chthonic (subterranean) structures (Hypogeum of Hal-Saflieni).

Ancient Egypt (3050–332 BCE): Spanning three main kingdoms and several millennia, Ancient Egyptian architecture provided the core foundations for design with intricate measurement systems, detailed architectural drawings, and designated architects who were responsible for all aspects of a project. Their work grew more refined and continued to inspire future generations, leaving a lasting impact on the built world..

    Key sites: Temple of Hatshepsut (right), Temples of Luxor and Karnak, Abu Simbel

Classical (850 BCE–476 CE): The Ancient Greeks developed planned cities with well-ordered urban grids to control the movement of people and future growth. Nearby, in what is now Italy, a group called the Etruscans introduced the arch, which Ancient Roman architects adapted to build aqueducts, triumphal arches, stadia like the Colosseum, and domed structures. In the east, Buddhist architecture flourished in the forms of earthen stupas and wooden pagodas, among others.

    Key sites: Athenian Acropolis (left), Pantheon, Tōdai-ji, Ajanta Caves

Byzantine (330–15th century): Navigating sites in both Eastern Europe and Asia, architects from the Byzantine Empire merged forms and building types. Their domes were higher than those previously built and included vivid mosaics, rich carvings, and complex geometries to bring beauty to their buildings internally.

    Key sites: Basilica of San Vitale, St. Mark's Basilica, Hagia Sophia (right)

Mesoamerican (1800 BCE–1521 CE): Central American city-states flourished through vast urban centers that were designed around solar and astronomical alignments, framed by richly painted towering temples and recreational complexes.

Key sites: Teotihuacán, Tikal, Chichén Itzá (above)

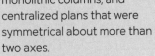

Gothic (1100–1450): Following the medieval period and its defensive structures, the Gothic era called for expanded urban planning. Cathedral building also began. These stone and timber structures had soaring, vaulted interior spaces supported by flying buttresses and light from stained glass windows.

Key figures: Maurice de Sully, Villard de Honnecourt, William of Sens

Romanesque (800–1100): Using Roman forms, architects of this era built Christian structures with thick, solid walls; monolithic columns; and centralized plans that were symmetrical about more than two axes.

Key sites: Aachen, Abbey of Sainte-Foy

Renaissance (mid-14th–16th centuries): As a rebirth of the Classical period and its architecture, architects took inspiration from the ancient world; a new mastery of perspective was essential to their designs. The wider availability of paper allowed architects to compile more sketchbooks and writings than ever before, and many of these works explored the orders of architecture: Tuscan, Doric, Ionic, Corinthian, and Composite.

Key figures: Filippo Brunelleschi, Leonardo da Vinci, Michelangelo, Andrea Palladio (right)

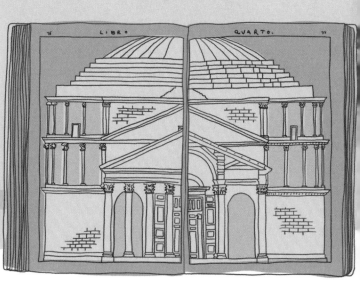

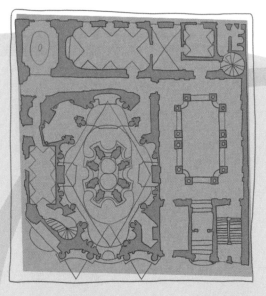

Baroque (late 16th–early 18th centuries): This era featured grand palaces and churches, with ostentatious displays of wealth and artistic craft. With complicated plans featuring concave and convex forms, the interiors also included carved decorations, mirrors, and trompe-l'oeil (trick of the eye) techniques to captivate occupants with rich colors and surfaces.

Key figures: Gian Lorenzo Bernini, Francesco Borromini (left), Guarino Guarini, Balthasar Neumann, Sir Christopher Wren

Neoclassicism (18th–19th centuries): With growing interest in science and archaeological discoveries in Pompeii, Greece, Egypt, and Syria, some Western architects undertook The Grand Tour, traveling to these newly unearthed sites to study them. With new knowledge of the ancient world and growing urban populations, majestic new building typologies developed in Europe during this time, such as opera houses, libraries, and museums.

Key figures: Giovanni Battista Piranesi, Sir John Soane, Benjamin Henry Latrobe, Henri Labrouste

Gothic Revival (18th–19th centuries): Taking inspiration from Gothic architecture, architects in the United Kingdom began using new materials, such as cast iron and large panes of glass, to build foreboding structures.

Key figures: Horace Walpole (above), Augustus Welby Northmore Pugin

Arts & Crafts (late 19th and early 20th centuries): This movement was characterized by a reaction to the loss of craft as the result of rapid industrialization and the mechanization of construction methods. Seeking a balance, architects and artisans collaborated to make mass-produced objects such as furniture, wallpaper, and other textiles.

Key figures: William Morris, C. F. A. Voysey, Mary Seton Watts

Art Nouveau (late 19th and early 20th centuries):

This short-lived movement is considered the first true modern decorative style manifested in architecture, typography, graphic illustration, furniture, jewelry, and the decorative arts, such as furniture and other objects. Its characteristic feature is the use of the whiplash or arabesque: graceful lines careening around a printed page, on a poster, or winding through a space, like a plant's vines.

Key figures: Antoni Gaudí, Hector Guimard, Victor Horta, Charles Rennie Mackintosh, Macdonald Sisters

Art Deco (1925–1940):

Filled with sharply angled forms, zigzag shapes, and implied movement, this style captured the feeling of electricity and radio waves. With a palette of aluminum, black lacquer, and glass, the works were often called Jazz Modern.

Key figures: Raymond Hood, William Van Alen (right)

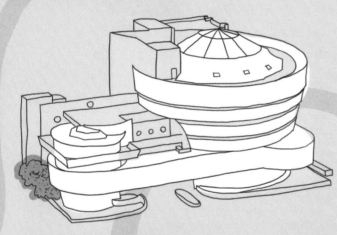

Modernism (1900s to 1960s):

Sites of industrial production in the Western world fueled new developments in structure, new materials, and design initiatives focused on workers' movements and housing. Architects integrated design processes based on mass production. Concrete became popular for the first time since the Ancient Roman era. Steel and glass were also essential, with minimal use of decoration.

Key figures: Lina Bo Bardi, Charles and Ray Eames, Eileen Gray, Walter Gropius, Louis Kahn, Charlotte Perriand, Frank Lloyd Wright (above)

Postmodernism (1970s to early 21st century):

This style reintroduced several early modern concepts, such as ornament, iconography, and pluralism. Postmodern structures are often dramatic stylistic hybrids that mix forms and references from different periods. For example, Egyptian pyramids were reimagined in glass and steel, and brightly painted columns and playful oversize sculptures were integrated into civic buildings that were stoic and stately in previous eras.

Key figures: Michael Graves, Charles Jencks, Aldo Rossi, Robert Venturi, Denise Scott Brown

CHALLENGES IN ARCHITECTURE

As professionals, architects balance the practical needs of a society with artistry, so they must be simultaneously pragmatic and visionary. How can architects juggle these seemingly opposite and competing interests?

One of the most incredible aspects of architecture is also its biggest challenge: There is not one right method or solution for architectural design. Instead, architecture is a compelling puzzle of options that requires the analysis of both what can be done and what the obstacles are in doing it.

Climate change and technology are at the forefront of today's challenges. Following the Industrial Revolution, architects, engineers, and civic leaders turned to new architectural programs and building typologies to meet the needs of rapidly growing urban populations, pioneering

ARCHITECTS ARE ...

- Creative problem-solvers who see challenges as opportunities
- Inquisitive about their surroundings and able to explore concepts from multiple perspectives
- Makers and active collaborators
- Willing to experiment and take risks in their design work, and demonstrate resilience in the face of both constructive criticism and adversity
- Attentive to craft, ensuring their work reflects the time, research, and revision they invested to develop a project
- Able to communicate in a clear and compelling manner through visual material as well as written and verbal presentations

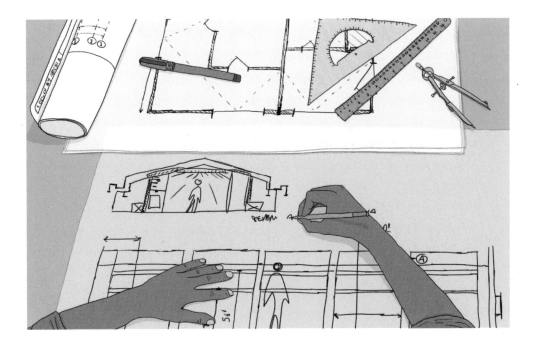

large-scale projects that involved an unprecedented approach to city planning. Architects and builders consumed massive quantities of energy to extract materials from the earth, move them to sites across the globe, and construct forms that used water, electricity, and fuel in new ways.

Today's architects are addressing our past energy consumption and taking sustainable approaches to the built environment. Technology is now helping us fight climate change with smart building systems and monitoring programs to ensure efficiency in building design, construction, and operation.

But we have to ensure that the practice of architecture does not succumb to increasing automation. Although computer modeling and robotic systems can be integral to strengthening design, we still need architects to consider the idiosyncratic aspects of buildings and building sites and to cultivate beauty within their designs. In our increasingly complicated world that is full of unique building types and new ways of sharing information, architects also have to weigh the benefits of being a

20 FAMOUS ARCHITECTS

1. **Imhotep** (27th century BCE): One of the first recorded architects in written history, he designed the Step Pyramid at Saqqārah that inspired monumental constructions across the globe.

2. **Marcus Vitruvius Pollio** (c. 90–20 BCE): Roman engineer, military strategist, and architect, he wrote *De architectura* (1st century BCE), the first-known treatise on architecture.

3. **Michelangelo** (1475–1564): As a painter, sculptor, and architect, he helped enliven and redesign Renaissance Rome under the patronage of various popes.

4. **Mimar Sinan** (c. 1488–1588): The foremost architect of the Ottoman Empire, he created nearly 200 structures.

5. **Andrea Palladio** (1508–1580): This stonecutter reshaped the landscape of the Veneto region through the design of churches, palaces, and villas, but his most important contribution was a 1570 treatise known as the *I Quattro Libri dell'- Architettura* (The Four Books on Architecture).

6. **Thomas Jefferson** (1743–1826): Although he was self-trained, Jefferson's work as a designer and advocate within the nation's government shaped early American architecture and its reliance on Classical forms.

7. **Antoni Gaudí** (1852–1926): Inspired by nature, Gaudí's structures defy gravity while seamlessly integrating sculpture and color. He also pioneered the use of the catenary arch.

8. **Frank Lloyd Wright** (1867–1959): An inexhaustible American architect, he designed projects in the United States and Japan, taking inspiration from organic forms and patterns.

9. **Ludwig Mies van der Rohe** (1886–1969): After leaving the Bauhaus, he helped introduce modernism to the United States as a master of details with glass and steel. He is known for his philosophy "less is more."

10. **Marion Mahony Griffin** (1871–1961): The first licensed female architect in recorded history, she practiced in the United States, India, and Australia, where she co-designed the capital city of Canberra.

11. **Le Corbusier** (1887–1965): Born Charles-Édouard Jeanneret, he pioneered the L'Esprit Nouveau through paintings, "machines for living," bold urban plans, and various publications such as the transformative *Vers une Architecture* (1923) [Toward an Architecture].

12. **Paul Revere Williams** (1894–1980): A prolific designer on the West Coast, he broke the color barrier within the American Institute of Architects (AIA) as both the first Black member and the recipient of an AIA Gold Medal (posthumously).

13. **Lina Bo Bardi** (1914–1992): A leading modernist with a distinctive drawing style, she was an industrial designer, architect, and social advocate who took inspiration from regional vernacular designs and landscapes.

14. **Norma Merrick Sklarek** (1926–2012): Hurdling gender, color, and architectural licensing obstacles throughout her career, she designed large-scale federal structures in the United States and abroad, and she later founded her own firm with two other women.

15. **I. M. Pei** (1917–2019): Renowned for both skyscrapers and cultural icons, his work was characterized by triangulation and the use of space frames.

16. **Frank Gehry** (b. 1929): A pioneer in deconstructivism, Gehry blurs the lines between architecture and sculpture.

17. **Tadao Ando** (b. 1941): Attentive to the art of casting concrete, he complements a simple material palette with bold forms and dramatic plays of light.

18. **Dame Zaha Hadid** (1950–2016): With intersecting angles and curvaceous volumes, her architecture redefined structural expressionism, and she was the first female to receive the prestigious Pritzker Prize. Her work frequently used parametric design, which is based on computational algorithms.

19. **Kazuyo Seijima** (b. 1956): Co-founder of the innovative firm SANAA, her work tests the limits of lightness and transparency in architecture.

20. **David Adjaye** (b. 1966): An artist, photographer, and architect with an international practice steeped in both museum and residential design, he draws on his Ghanaian roots for inspiration.

specialist within the field versus being a generalist. Architects can pursue either path, but with so many options and technologies in our modern world, it is difficult to be both.

It's essential that architects ensure their buildings better the lives of people from different income levels, backgrounds, and geographic regions. Unfortunately, architectural history is full of examples of buildings and urban layouts that excluded certain populations, so today's designers are tackling affordability, social change, and environmental concerns. These challenges are daunting, but exciting.

ARCHITECTURE TODAY

Does architecture sound like an exciting field, full of options and explorations? Great! So, what next? If you are interested in architecture, one of the most important and valuable things you can do is sharpen your skills in visual observation. Notice your surroundings and investigate situations where certain spaces or architectural details seem really compelling, or even really unsuccessful. Start drawing and recording your interpretations and ideas. Can you imagine a way to solve a problem in the built environment? It can be as small as redesigning a doorknob that is difficult to grasp or as big as planning an entire city. How can you represent your idea on paper or with a physical or digital model? Your first steps toward a career in design can start with just a few actions: looking, questioning, drawing, and making.

Before thinking about a college program or what incredible awards your first built project will earn, check out ArchCareersGuide.com to learn about the different paths to becoming a licensed architect. The site includes an extensive list of summer architecture programs at design organizations and schools across the United States and even abroad. These programs are varied. Some are residential, meaning you stay in dorms or other provided housing, whereas others are day camps, but they all provide the invaluable opportunity to experience an architectural studio in person. You will learn what it is like to complete a design charette, a meeting of project stakeholders to solve a problem. You will also learn about a jury, which is a constructive critique of your work. If you attend an architecture camp or design school, you will get previews of the exercises you could undertake in the professional world.

You can also look up your local American Institute of Architects (AIA) chapter and see if they have open events or if an architect would be willing to serve as a mentor. This book has a list of resources (see page 103) for texts, films, blogs, and even free software that will expand and engage your interests and help you build new knowledge and skills. With so much to investigate, shall we begin?

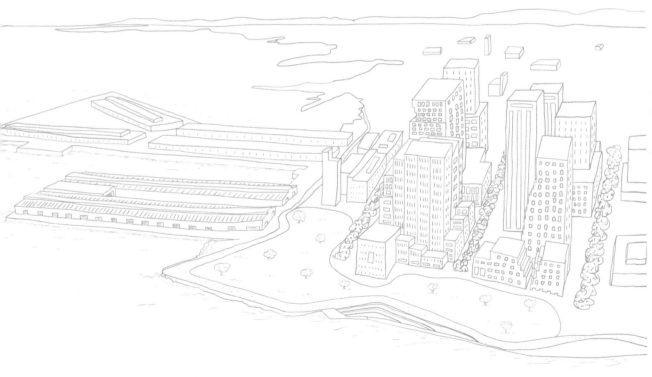

INSIDE AN ARCHITECT'S
MESSENGER BAG

To get a glimpse into contemporary architectural practice, let's look inside an architect's messenger bag. This accessory is great because it allows you to easily carry some necessary tools, including:

- A sketchbook, a few drawing instruments, and maybe a tablet for digital sketching
- A laptop to make digital models and project presentations, while using budget spreadsheets and contracts to keep track of a project's timeline and deliverables
- A phone and headphones to correspond with clients and project collaborators, plus some good music to enjoy while designing
- A camera (or even just a smartphone)—you never know when you will find inspiration
- A thermos with a favorite drink
- A tape measure, a hard hat, sturdy shoes, and sunglasses for construction site visits

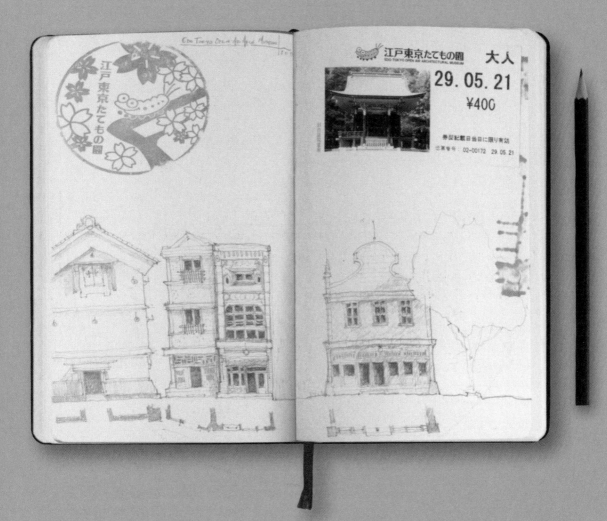

Chapter 2
HOW ARCHITECTS SHAPE STRUCTURES

AS DESIGNERS, WE LIVE IN EXCITING TIMES. New materials and technologies enable us to build practically anything we can dream up (if we have the money).

Across the globe, there are various sites with teams of architects and engineers in a race to the sky, trying to develop the tallest building. The Great Pyramid of Giza held the honor as the tallest building in the world for nearly 4,000 years. But since the Industrial Revolution, rarely has a structure held the coveted title of "tallest" for more than a decade. In the 1950s, Frank Lloyd Wright imagined a mile-high skyscraper. As of the summer of 2020, the Burj Khalifa in Dubai, UAE (built in 2010), is the tallest structure in the world at 2,717 feet. We are about halfway to Wright's vision, but several other structures are quickly rising!

Skyscrapers are iconic buildings that pierce the clouds and inspire architectural advancements, but they are not the only architectural wonders worthy of our study. It's important for us to investigate how other buildings solve problems and advance society.

For example, the National Museum of African American History and Culture (NMAAHC) is perhaps the greenest new museum. Located in Washington, D.C., the project responds to its famous surroundings and significant structures within the nation's capital city, like the Lincoln Memorial, Vietnam Veterans Memorial, the Washington Monument, the White House, and the Thomas Jefferson Memorial. With such famous architectural neighbors, the NMAAHC took a new approach to design in the capital city, using different materials and patterns while rethinking how a museum can also serve as a memorial and a resource for the community.

Completed in 2016, the project is a model of collaboration, and it won a number of national and international design awards. Led by Freelon Adjaye Bond/SmithGroup, the design team worked with curators and leaders from the Smithsonian Institution to create a new kind of museum. With a portion of the museum buried in the earth, visitors literally pass from light to dark during their progression through the museum's floors. Although the structure has a whimsical appearance and dramatic shadows, it is still built to withstand any seismic activity in the area.

The National Museum of African American History and Culture

The project is also a model of sustainability and was certified LEED (U.S. Green Building Council's Leadership in Energy and Environmental Design) Gold, a green rating system discussed later in this chapter. The main goal of systems like LEED is to introduce collaboration across disciplines early in a project to create structures that consider the natural environment and the health and happiness of the community.

Through these design principles, the NMAAHC uses the sun for ample daylighting and views of the National Mall. For artificial light, solar panels help power the building. It has systems that enhance the air quality, and the project's design reduces light pollution to create healthier surroundings. The museum reduces water use through low-flow fixtures and the reuse of gently used water, called greywater, from sinks for efficient landscape irrigation. Through careful planning and management, almost half the building is composed of local or recycled materials, and nearly 80 percent of the construction waste was recycled. Best of all, the museum charges no admission fee, so it is accessible to the whole community.

DEEP DIVE

No matter the project type or size, it takes a number of steps for architects and their teams to bring a project to life. At the initial stages of a project, architects complete project briefings and program (building use) review. Here, they participate in community and stakeholder meetings to learn about initial project goals, highlighting key features and questions. They determine the scope of work for a project and begin research to determine useful precedents. They explore the site in order to understand constraints and opportunities, such as environmental factors like climate and soil conditions and cultural considerations like how the building will respond to its surroundings.

For example, a building in an area prone to earthquakes may need to have deep foundations for dampeners, whereas a structure in a historic area may need to have a different foundation and overall site strategy because there might be archaeological remnants that need to be preserved for future study.

The project team carefully documents its work throughout all these stages, making visual and verbal presentations to clients in order to maintain an open line of communication about the project's prospects and parameters. Through frequent meetings and communications, the architect ensures that all invested parties are on the same page.

After the selection and approval of a scheme, projects move into the design development phase. This stage includes revising design ideas and producing more detailed models and drawings, both two- and three-dimensional. Project cost estimates are updated, and architects

FOUR STEPS TO DEVELOP A PROJECT

1. Begin schematic design, including initial ideas, sketches, and proposals. Project team members (such as engineers, landscape architects, technical consultants, and community members) investigate relevant building codes and explore different design proposals or concepts.
2. Build initial models and drawings that test different ideas.
3. Develop the project budget.
4. Conduct site surveys. Team members take detailed measurements, gather soil samples to understand the ground conditions, and record other significant features of the site, such as vegetation, water features, and topography. This phase also involves the proposal of overall sustainability goals. It's essential to establish goals for the sustainable production, operation, and maintenance of the building early in the project.

complete any necessary submittals (such as forms and drawings) for project registration and approval. They must compile and complete all the necessary paperwork for a project to get it approved for construction and, eventually, occupation.

Following final design review and the selection of materials, fixtures, and sometimes even furniture, architects prepare construction documents and any necessary shop drawings for specialized fabrication. They work with contractors who supervise different aspects of physically making the building and managing operations on the site. They also review field reports that detail project progress and any issues relating to the design as well as unforeseen circumstances such as weather events or unanticipated structural issues. During site visits when the project is under construction, architects supervise and review the construction process as well as necessary inspections and certifications, which are especially important for green-rating projects.

Sometimes the architect's work ends at construction, but often it includes seeing the project through commissioning, the earliest stages of its operations, and necessary project documentation, such as capturing photographs and videos. Project closeout can also include a post-occupancy assessment, which determines whether the project is performing as expected once the occupants have started using the building. This step is extremely important for projects with ambitious goals in environmental performance.

Above all, architects must always consider the health, safety, and welfare (HSW) of anyone who interacts with the building. Architects can make beautiful, functional spaces, but their main responsibility is to ensure the well-being of the building's occupants. They also need to make sure the structure beneficially responds to the needs of the immediate community and has an enriching, not detrimental, environmental footprint.

WHAT ARCHITECTS CAN DO

As noted by ancient architect Vitruvius, architecture has always been a multifaceted profession. Architects don't just design buildings; they can also create pieces of art and sculpture, graphic systems such as new typefaces, entire city plans and connective transportation infrastructure, and processes that integrate systems thinking. Let's explore some of the other things that architects can do.

Develop New Technology and Research

Since the beginning of design history, architects have used the built environment as a testing ground for advancing technology and fabrication. We can see this phenomenon in the use of post and lintel systems (like Stonehenge); arches, buttresses, and towering columns that support skyscrapers; and in complex systems that relied on simple machines, mechanical devices, and computer-controlled methods.

For example, the London-based DLA Scan Architectural Studio is pioneering the use of experimental photography and 3D laser scanning for surveying and interpreting the built environment, recording structures and landscape features with precise measurements. With this type of research, architects can respond to the challenges of a rapidly changing world by protecting significant cultural and historic sites (known as built heritage), mitigating the impacts of natural and human-made disasters, and pioneering positive urban regeneration projects that help revive underused and underdeveloped areas in cities.

Drive Disaster Response and Recovery

After a tornado, an earthquake, a hurricane, or another disaster, architects can be some of the first boots on the ground to help communities assess damage, recover, and rebuild. Through the American Institute of Architects (AIA), architects can undergo special training so they can volunteer to assist other agencies in times of need and rebuild in ways that minimize the impact of future disasters. Nonprofit organizations such

Shigeru Ban's Paper Cathedral

as the Open Architecture Collaborative and Architects Without Borders work to design and build emergency housing, community centers, and mobile clinics.

Architects also think about ways to mitigate human-made disasters and accidents. For example, federal projects such as courthouses and departmental agency headquarters around the United States are designed with a secure perimeter that keeps a blast or attempted security breach away from the critical structural elements of the building. Although these security measures are important, we don't want our cities to be full of fortified structures that look like a revival of the medieval period, so architects have to ensure that the barriers are minimally invasive and feel like they are part of the overall site design, rather than modern-day ramparts.

Contribute to Human Health

In response to the COVID-19 pandemic, architects collaborated virtually to design and implement solutions for hospital shortages, helping convert civic and convention centers into temporary medical sites. They also reimagined space layouts within schools, universities, and offices to accommodate social-distancing guidelines.

Formerly developed sites, especially those with industrial uses, are often compromised with hazardous materials, chemicals, or other contaminants. There are nearly half a million brownfield (industrially polluted) sites in the United States. Before these sites can be redeveloped, they have to be carefully documented, studied, and cleaned to avoid causing major human health issues. By redeveloping these abandoned and contaminated sites, we can bring new life to places that were once important and vibrant, especially in urban centers along waterfronts and key transportation corridors. Using brownfields also ensures the preservation of undeveloped open land and habitats. Architects and landscape architects with the organizations D.I.R.T. studio and HILLWORKS work extensively with brownfield redevelopment, urban regeneration, and Superfund projects that are located in particularly toxic sites.

Fight Rising Sea Levels

Architects can work on innovative, large-scale infrastructure projects such as tunnels, bridges, dams, and coastal barriers. Climate change threatens coastal cities and sites across the globe, so architects are proposing new ways to approach construction and environmental conservation. For example, the unprecedented MOSE Project in Venice strives to combat sea-level rise with operable gates that will protect the Venetian Lagoon from the rising tides of the Adriatic Sea. Projects like these have the potential to connect and preserve coastal cities everywhere.

Make Temporary Architecture Sustainable

The New York–based design practice The Living used biological systems and unconventional building materials in their work for a project called "Hy-Fi," a temporary installation and summer concert venue for MoMA PS1 in Queens. From a distance, the project looked like a series of circular masonry towers, but upon closer inspection, visitors could see that the bricks were actually made of biodegradable materials. Temporary architecture and exhibit design have been used since the 1800s, but these short-term projects can be costly, both financially and environmentally. The Living's project was one of the first to actively question how a building's materials could truly return to the earth in a safe and sustainable way.

Make Tourism Sustainable

This book explores sites all over the world, and it is essential for architects to deepen their knowledge of the built and natural world through travel. But it's also important to consider the environmental footprint of tourism and how we can leave sites better than we found them. Places like Venice, Italy, have been overrun with tourists who contribute to the economy but also cause substantial wear to the historic city and its iconic structures while also taxing the city infrastructure, from the use

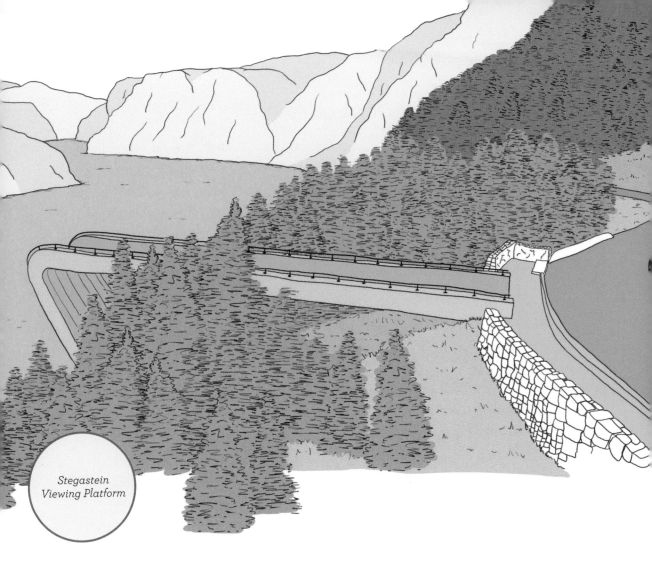

*Stegastein
Viewing Platform*

of fresh water to the management of waste from restaurants and hotels. To address more sustainable approaches to tourism and make visitors more cognizant of their impact, certain architects design structures that introduce ecotourism into the built environment. Buildings can be essential conduits for conservation. In Norway, various architects contributed projects along the Norwegian Scenic Route, a series of 18 highways winding along breathtaking fjords, mountains, and valleys. Architects created observation decks and buildings to support tourism such as restaurants, hotels, and rest stops. Many of the buildings are small in scale but have a huge impact, using local materials and touching the earth lightly to focus visitors' attention on the unparalleled landscapes.

Design Everyday Objects

Sometimes, architects work within the field of industrial design, which is the creation, development, and fabrication of objects for mass production. For example, Zaha Hadid designed experimental shoes, Thomas Heather-wick's studio created eco-friendly buses for London, and Michael Graves produced a housewares line with Target. A number of architects are also well known for their furniture design, especially chairs. Check out the collections of the Vitra Design Museum.

Turn Imagination into Physical and Virtual Worlds

Even in our technologically advanced world, it is hard to imagine architecture without drawing and modeling. Both are tied to the concept of visualization, when we represent an idea in two or three dimensions for others to understand and explore. This ability to translate imagination into reality allows architects to work on a wide range of built products, including theater and movie sets, museums, and even video game environments. Who better to envision a virtual environment than an architect?

CAREERS IN ARCHITECTURE

With all that an architect can do, it's no surprise that the profession has a number of specializations. Architects specialize in certain building programs (how we use a space), material and fabrication systems, and structural methods. They can also focus on a particular region, climate, or style. But regardless of their area within the field of architecture, an architect needs to be inquisitive and collaborative and never stop learning or testing the limits of design. It's also important to know that architectural offices can be very different in terms of scope (what they work on) and size (how many people are employed). Some firms are professional microcosms, meaning they employ different types of architects, engineers, and interior designers, as well as a range of other disciplines, such as graphic and web designers, marketing and advertising specialists, office managers, lawyers, and accountants. Smaller firms typically have design specialties and often rely on consultants and other project partners.

Residential Architects

Residential architects ask themselves how to design a welcoming and comfortable home that contributes to a healthy environment. One of the reasons a specialty in residential architecture is so important is that humans spend about 90 percent of their time indoors, especially at home, where they eat, sleep, relax, study, and work. Unlike in an office, a school, or a hospital, the daily activities in a home are extremely varied. Residential architects are uniquely qualified to tackle the challenge of designing and reshaping the most personal spaces we inhabit. The self-designed homes of architects are some of the famous, inventive experiments in residential architecture. Check out the residences of Thomas Jefferson, Sir John Soane, Alvar and Aino Aalto, Charles and Ray Eames, Richard Rogers, and Jennifer Bonner.

Think about how we define "home." The word has a pretty broad definition and means something different to everyone, and residential

Atlanta's
*Haus Gables by
Jennifer Bonner*

architects work at multiple scales. One project could be a single-family residence, like a house, while others are for many families, such as duplexes, townhouses, and apartments. These architects can even work on larger-scale community housing projects, such as university dorms, condominiums, and assisted-living facilities like nursing homes and live-in rehabilitation centers.

Residential architects produce new and renovated constructions, rethinking life at home and responding to design trends, as well as adapting homes for accessibility or the needs of an aging occupant. They also evaluate a home's energy consumption to make it more efficient and cost-effective, creating a healthier environment for the inhabitants and the planet through a reduced annual carbon footprint.

Commercial Architects

An architect's client can be an individual project owner, the users of the building, or a larger brand or company. Within residential architecture, the client is typically the homeowner and inhabitant, but for commercial architecture, we can think of the client as a company that provides services to its users. Commercial architects design for retail stores, restaurants, hotels, entertainment venues, office spaces, health-care facilities, and many other businesses.

Commercial architects work on eye-catching structures that attract people to stores and express a company's identity or culture, ensuring that the structure and aesthetics reflect a particular style. For example, the British architecture firm Foster + Partners has worked with Apple on a number of their flagship and retail stores around the world. One of their most recent collaborations was the Apple Store in Chicago, which uses a simple cube form with sleek, laminated glass supports and an impossibly thin roof of carbon fiber. The building itself is like Apple's products: It uses materials in innovative ways, with an aesthetic that features the clean lines and curved edges the company is known for.

The Apple
Store Chicago
by Foster +
Partners

When fashion meets architecture, designers carefully consider branding (the underlying identity, values, and ambitions of a company) and user experience. The spaces that commercial architects create within stores feature integrated displays reflective of the brand's aesthetics and ideals. Architects consider how the building's interior materials will wear with customer use, as well as how certain aspects of the interior and storefront can be manipulated over time to cater to different seasons or changing trends.

Architects also work to direct the flow of customers within these commercial spaces to indicate where they enter, browse, and purchase goods. Famous shopping corridors around the world are some of the best places to see experimental and cutting-edge commercial architecture. To see this avant-garde architecture, check out famous areas such as Fifth Avenue in New York City and the Omotesandō and Ginza districts in Tokyo. Commercial architects also consider how design and materials can reshape how we see well-established brands. For example, Ross Barney Architects created a flagship store for McDonald's in Chicago that showcases mass timber, a growing movement in sustainable architecture that uses engineered wood and atypical wall systems to reduce carbon footprints.

Industrial Architects

We often think of architects designing the structures that people interact with on a regular basis, including houses, offices, stores, religious buildings, and sites for learning, such as schools, museums, and libraries. But architects are also responsible for the structures that fuel our world in terms of production and distribution. Industrial architects work on large-scale projects that are typically not open to the public but that are essential to everyday life. They design factories, power plants, refineries, and warehouses. These projects are complex because they often deal with high-energy operations and sensitive products or situations, such as chemicals or intense temperatures and pressure.

Since the 1700s, architects have been designing factories that not only streamline labor, but also improve the experience of the workers. Claude Nicolas Ledoux designed the Royal Saltworks at Arc-et-Senans in France, now a UNESCO World Heritage site. The factory was also the site of an idealized planned city where workers and their families lived. Architect and engineer Albert Kahn worked with American automaker Henry Ford to design company structures with the world's first assembly lines, which became a key feature in the American Industrial Revolution.

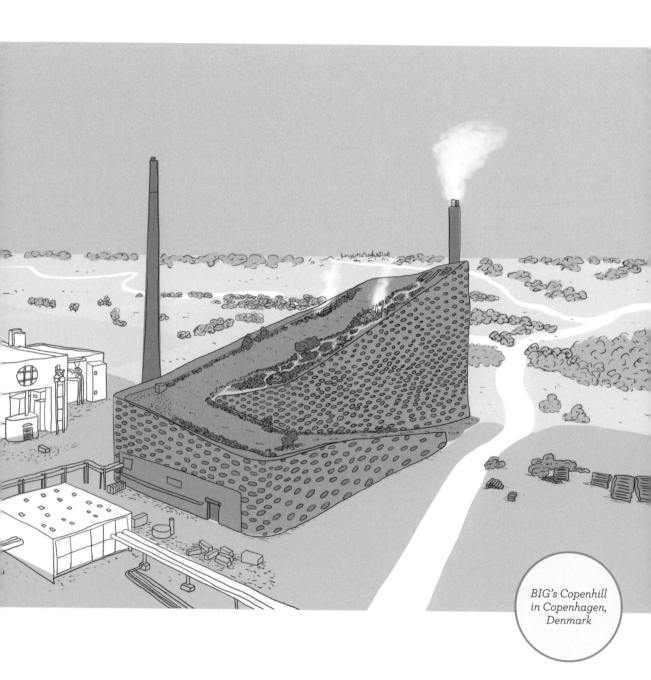

BIG's Copenhill
in Copenhagen,
Denmark

Today's industrial architects are rising to environmental and social challenges to design power plants that move away from fossil fuels and toward renewable energy like hydroelectric power stations, biomass power plants, and other innovative structures. For example, designers in Iceland harness geothermal energy to power the greenhouses that feed the island nation. And just outside Copenhagen, Denmark, architects built the CopenHill, a structure that converts waste to energy while simultaneously serving as a ski slope.

In the 21st century, we can also think of computers as both factories and power plants. To keep online systems and cloud services running smoothly, architects design data centers that keep the massive amounts of computational equipment and processors cool.

Architects in Historic Preservation

Some architects specialize in the historic built environment, working with existing structures that are important for understanding place, time, and human interaction. Their work may focus on small structures, such as the preservation of an 18th-century privy (outdoor toilet), a residence, or large-scale structures such as bridges, factories, or entire neighborhoods.

Architects who work in the field of historic preservation are interested in how we protect the built record of the past, but they are also concerned with how these buildings and sites are important parts of present-day communities and development initiatives. In order to understand the work of these designers, we need to define a few specific terms: preservation, restoration, reconstruction, and rehabilitation. These four approaches are key to working within historic environments, and each employs specific tools.

PRESERVATION

Preservation, known in some countries as conservation, is the least invasive approach. Architects focus on sustaining the historic property and its materials. Some structural work may be necessary to stabilize the

Richardson-Olmsted Campus restoration in Buffalo, New York

building, but new additions or changes to the form are not acceptable. The architect may update some of the building's features—such as plumbing, electrical, and mechanical systems—to make it more accessible and functional. The building may also require changes to ensure that it is legally occupiable and in compliance with any local building codes.

RESTORATION

Restoration takes preservation a bit further, as the architect works to restore a property to a selected time or significant period. This approach is like creating a snapshot of what the building once looked like. The architect may need to remove certain elements or materials that were later additions, and they may have to add new elements to ensure it resembles a certain form or character.

RECONSTRUCTION

Reconstruction involves substantial new construction to reproduce a site or project that has not survived. There may be some fragments or archaeological elements, as well as information from archives such as photographs or written descriptions. These projects may be constructed on the original site or in a different location (even a museum). The architect may choose to use historic methods of construction or more advanced technology, such as 3D printing, to replicate elements.

REHABILITATION

Rehabilitation, also known as adaptive reuse, means converting a historic structure or site into a new use, bringing new life and economic prosperity to the site. There may be some substantial alterations, but the site still maintains chief aspects of its historical character.

Gensler's Gusto in San Francisco, California

Interior Architects

Interior architects are sometimes confused with interior designers, but they pursue different types of professional certification, such as the National Council for Interior Design Qualification (NCIDQ) versus the Architectural Registration Exam (ARE). Because of differences in their degree programs, internships, and testing, interior architects can manipulate structural elements within buildings, as well as parts of a project that interface with mechanical, electrical, and plumbing systems. An interior designer may focus on the more qualitative aspects of a space—how it feels in terms of surfaces and textures—whereas an interior architect would also explore how that space performs in terms of energy efficiency and indoor air quality. Both professions work in specialized subcategories, such as residences, commercial spaces, offices, retail spaces, and hospitality interiors like hotels and restaurants.

In terms of project phases and scope, there is some overlap between the professions. For example, both interior designers and interior architects select many of the soft aspects of a project, such as the textiles, floor coverings, and furnishings. While working on a project, both may explore the hardware, such as doorknobs and cabinet pulls, as well as the lighting, whether moveable pieces or those fixed to walls or ceilings.

Many architectural firms, such as SOM and Perkins + Will, have distinct interior architecture departments. These divisions focus on the interior aesthetic and layout of spaces. They may work on a new building, but it is quite common for interior architects to work on projects that renovate and update existing interior spaces, such as converting an office during a change of owners or updating the space to respond to different technical or collaborative conditions. Interior architects can also help museums configure new arrangements to accommodate different acquisitions or unique approaches to exhibit design.

ANDREW DALEY, AIA

REGISTERED ARCHITECT, SENIOR ASSOCIATE AT SHOP ARCHITECTS
IN NEW YORK CITY, AND FORMER LECTURER IN ARCHITECTURE
AT THE TAUBMAN COLLEGE OF ARCHITECTURE AND URBAN PLANNING
AT THE UNIVERSITY OF MICHIGAN

What do you do?

I work on diplomatic projects around the world for the U.S. Department of State's Office of Overseas Building Operations, and my two most recent projects were embassies: one in Honduras and one in Thailand. We focus on how these structures showcase different approaches to materials, the climates, and the influence of local sites while dealing with complex security concerns.

What does a typical workday look like?

I typically get to the office early to get ahead on things. I spend time in meetings, on calls, reviewing drawings and specifications, monitoring project progress, and coordinating between different groups on the project team.

Why did you want to be an architect?

From the time I could talk, I've apparently said that I wanted to make buildings. No one in my family is an architect, no one from my high school became an architect, and my guidance counselor didn't really know what to do with me, so I was on my own exploring paths. I was always interested in how things work and construction processes—it is like a big puzzle.

Where did you go to school?

I went to the University of Virginia for my Bachelor of Science in Architecture, then Rice University for my Master of Architecture. Between programs, I took two years off to work in practice and on a design/build project. For the first two years of my undergraduate architectural education, I really wasn't focused on studio, and that set me back a bit. But by the time I went to graduate school, I had more focus and knew what I wanted to pursue.

What has been the most challenging part about being an architect?

Last year, I calculated that about 10 percent of my time was spent in transit. I go to Washington, D.C., a few times a month for meetings, and then on an international trip at least once per quarter for other meetings and site visits. With time zone shifts, this can make for long hours and an odd schedule. I also think it's really important to be part of a positive shift within the profession—it isn't about making it difficult for the next generation of designers because that's how you were trained. I want to uplift the people on my team and help them do their best work, so I work hard to be a good manager and take myself out of decisions. You can't take revisions, budget changes, or differences of design opinions personally, even though you invest so much time and energy in a project. You have to work to be open and objective, and that's hard.

What's your favorite/the most rewarding part about being an architect?

Celebrating a completed work is pretty exciting. As a project manager, one of my main tasks is facilitating communication for all the moving parts of a project. There are literally hundreds of people who work together to take a building to completion, especially at the scale of projects I've been working on lately. Seeing all those people and efforts come together is really rewarding.

What advice would you give to someone who's thinking about becoming an architect?

I would encourage a student to explore a broad education and be well-rounded. Some of the best designers I know came from different fields before they explored architecture, and they have such a unique perspective. If they are focused specifically on architecture, I would encourage them to also explore computer science, virtual reality, and parametric computation. All are related to visualization and the built environment.

PASCALE SABLAN, AIA, NOMA, LEED AP

**REGISTERED ARCHITECT, ASSOCIATE AT ADJAYE ASSOCIATES,
AND FOUNDER & EXECUTIVE DIRECTOR OF
BEYOND THE BUILT ENVIRONMENT, LLC; THE 315TH LIVING
BLACK FEMALE ARCHITECT IN THE UNITED STATES**

What does a typical workday look like?

I have multiple roles during my day. From about 9 a.m. to 6 p.m., my time is dedicated to my role at S9, managing all different aspects of practicing architecture for projects in the United States and abroad. Then I spend time every day from about 6 to 9 p.m. on architectural advocacy, including interviews, presentations, writing for various blogs and publications, podcasts, work in the community, and a lot more. In the LLC I founded, Beyond the Built Environment, we collaborate with different stakeholders and amplify their voices and methods for making equitable environments.

Why did you want to be an architect?

When I was in middle school, I was commissioned to complete a mural at the Pomonok Community Center in Queens. While I was working on my multicultural jungle gym design, a gentleman stopped by and said, "Hey, you can draw a straight line without a ruler. That's a good skill for an architect!" I don't think I had been exposed to the idea of being an architect before then, so it was just a casual comment from a stranger that inspired my curiosity to learn more about the profession.

Where did you go to school?

I completed a Bachelor of Architecture at Pratt Institute and then, just a few weeks after graduation, I began a Master of Science in Advanced Architectural Design at Columbia University. Both my degrees are in architecture because that is the path I knew I wanted to pursue. My goal is to make meaningful, socially responsible architecture that integrated communities into the design process and reflected different voices in the project.

What has been the most challenging part about being an architect?

As an architect, you are constantly learning and adapting to different places, groups of people, technology, and a whole array of issues. It isn't a career like my mom's—she's an accountant and she knows what each of her Wednesdays will look like! There are also some systemic barriers in architecture for women and people of color. This isn't just within the profession, but it also appears in the inequitable disparities of architecture in our cities and communities—who we build for and where we build. We need to dismantle these hurdles and make sure the profession and the practice of architecture reflect all the diversity in this world.

What's your favorite/the most rewarding part about being an architect?

Well, in many ways, it would be the same answer as the last question: As an architect, you're constantly learning.

What advice would you give to someone who's thinking about becoming an architect?

There are a number of great programs to get involved with to further your interests, and you should explore them as soon as possible. For example, there is the NOMA Project Pipeline Program, ACE Mentoring Program, and AIA's K-12 Initiatives. You should leverage your local resources: Get to know the architects and the builders, put a face to a name, and expand your research into their other work. Go visit construction sites with a mentor and get involved in seeing the practice of architecture. School is about learning about design; the profession is about making all the collaborations and systems work.

SUSTAINABILITY IN ARCHITECTURE

Sustainable architecture has several key features. It aims to reduce or eliminate greenhouse gas emissions, reduce energy use, minimize freshwater use by recycling greywater, minimize the production of waste, protect natural environments and important cultural sites, and foster a healthy environment for all living things in and around the building. Sustainability isn't just about adding solar panels or wind turbines to a project to check a box for environmental compliance. Truly green design is a comprehensive approach to the built environment that assesses not only energy consumption, but a whole range of additional issues. For example, how does the building use natural capital? We do not have inexhaustible natural resources, and if we create a building that performs well in terms of energy but uses nonrenewable materials for the structure or interior finishes or is built within a sensitive ecosystem, the building isn't really that green. Architects invested in genuinely sustainable design also have to evaluate a building's use of human capital. Is the building made with fair and safe labor practices? Are all the materials and systems beneficial to human health? Does maintaining the building put unnecessary physical or financial pressures on the owners or occupants? As you can see, there are a lot of variables, and it certainly is not easy to be green. But it is absolutely essential that architects work toward a fully sustainable future within the built environment.

Within the practice of architecture, green building is no longer an option or desirable perk for a project. Sustainable tenets and practices are now integrated with architectural education and part of the rigorous National Architectural Accrediting Board (NAAB) process that colleges and universities undergo to deliver the curriculum related to a professional degree in architecture. Sustainable design principles are also part of the Architectural Registration Exam (ARE) and various other design certifications that architects pursue to qualify their expertise in green design, such as LEED. We will learn much more about the many acronyms of architecture (such as NAAB, ARE, LEED) and the process of becoming an architect later.

Within sustainable architecture, we need to assess and design for the triple bottom line: the environment, the economy, and society. At the heart of this sustainable trio is the concept of systems thinking. All elements are intertwined, like an ecosystem, and certain decisions can have significant impacts on other elements of the system and their efficiency. Sustainable architecture is where design in the built environment meets biology, chemistry, and physics. But sustainable architecture is not just

PEOPLE
Social variables dealing with community, education, equality, social resources, health, well-being, and quality of life

BEARABLE

EQUITABLE

SUSTAINABLE

PLANET
Environmental variables relating to natural resources, water & air quality, energy conservation & land use

VIABLE

PROFIT
Economic variables dealing with the bottom line & cash flow

about science; it's also tied to society and the concept that a piece of truly green architecture should enhance its surrounding site and the lives of the people who interact with it. As architect William McDonough said, buildings cannot just be "less bad" but instead need to actively contribute to the quality of life for humans and the environment as a whole. He piloted the cradle-to-cradle approach, a form of life cycle assessment that we'll explore later in this book.

Designing for Climate

In order to address climate change, architects are working to limit natural resource depletion by relying on renewable materials and energy sources instead of fossil fuels. They also work to minimize the energy consumption of their buildings through efficient design and both active and passive systems.

An active system is any element (or collection of elements) that functions with moving parts and requires regular user input and external devices that usually need energy and maintenance. For example, a solar photovoltaic panel (PV) is an active solar device. Buildings can incorporater a number of other active renewable energy systems, such as wind, geothermal, hydroelectric, tidal, and biomass systems.

A passive system functions without moving parts or regular user input. For example, desert climates have substantial temperature fluctuations over a 24-hour period. Thick thermal mass walls can collect thermal energy from the sun over the course of the day, then slowly release this heat at night to passively warm a room.

Active and passive systems often work together effectively, so our desert room could also have a set of evacuated tubes on the roof that collect solar energy throughout the day to power a hot-water tank to provide us with a warm shower without using energy from the grid or a centralized power system. Many of the passive systems that are gaining momentum in the 21st century were actually integral to the pre-modern designs of indigenous and vernacular builders who honed their craft through time and experience rather than formal architectural education or practice.

To combat climate change, architects are also rejecting development in certain vulnerable places, such as wetlands, nature preserves, and otherwise undeveloped sites. But perhaps the most challenging aspect of responding to the impacts of climate change in the built environment is adapting existing structures and systems.

Architects are tackling new ways to insulate and condition (add heating and cooling) the energy-hungry buildings from the mid-20th century that are filled with glass. Architects are also pursuing ways of adapting existing structures and sites to be more resilient to rising sea levels, as well as the increasing frequency of extreme weather events such as tornados and hurricanes. By changing elements of their form, using different materials, incorporating barriers and wind breaks, and looking to the natural environment for inspiration, our buildings are better equipped to have longer and more effective life spans.

Energy Usage

Overall, it's estimated that buildings consume 40 percent of the world's energy. Although that's a huge number, we have to be careful that we do not automatically associate architecture, or industry, with bad environmental practices. Energy usage is shaped more by the choices made by people using buildings rather than the buildings themselves. When evaluating a building's efficiency in terms of energy usage, we have to look at two different forms of energy: expended and embodied.

Expended energy measures how much energy a building uses, and this type of energy is the easier of the two in terms of tracking and monitoring consumption. Embodied energy is the amount of energy it takes to make the building, from the fabrication of individual materials and the transportation of those materials to the building's site to the labor and construction practices needed to put the building together. As you can imagine, calculating embodied energy can be difficult. If we think about the energy used in a building as an equation, we would end up with a simple formula.

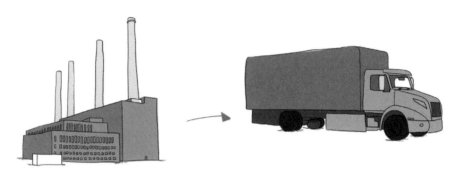

EMBODIED ENERGY (MAKING A BUILDING)
+
EXPENDED ENERGY (USING A BUILDING)
+
POST-USE = LIFE CYCLE ANALYSIS

With this formula, it's clear that to really understand how green a building is, we need to look at the entire building process. Making an energy-efficient building can be expensive, so architects, engineers, clients, and the community have to consciously invest in sustainability. Although the initial cost of the building may be higher to incorporate some active and passive systems that will reduce energy consumption, the operating costs of the building over its lifetime will be reduced. So it's important that architects fully highlight the payback of energy efficiency within their designs.

Sustainable Materials

The specific materials used in a building significantly contribute to its carbon footprint. The key tenet for the use of materials in a green building project is: reduce, reuse, recycle, and rethink. To assess the environmental footprint of a material, we need a full life cycle assessment. This information, often called a cradle-to-cradle assessment, includes where the material comes from, how the material is made, how it gets to the building site, how it is maintained, and what happens when it is no longer needed. Architects seek materials that are biodegradable, recyclable, and made from renewable resources and that have been manufactured in ways that do not damage the environment.

Within buildings, there is typically a mix of natural, synthetic, and composite materials. In addition to ensuring that the materials selected are aesthetically pleasing and durable, architects also have to ensure that the materials contain no toxins or volatile organic compounds (VOCs) that can off-gas over time and create poor indoor air quality. Selecting materials for a project involves much more than just selecting what looks good!

GREEN BUILDING STANDARDS

There are several rating systems for new constructions and renovation projects that encourage a holistic approach to the built environment, such as the United States Green Building Council's LEED (Leadership in Energy and Environmental Design) program, Green Globes for North America (adapted from the UK's BREEAM system), the WELL Building Standard, and the International Living Future Institute's Living Building Challenge. These systems encourage designers to integrate sustainable thinking into the earliest stages of a project. This means project partners collaborate frequently, and not just to address a particular question or install a system. The project moves through a thorough iterative process during which stakeholders weigh various options to make decisions and evaluate how those choices will impact other parts or phases of the project.

These rating systems reflect more than selection of green technologies and materials. They reflect a rethinking of design and construction processes by analyzing both the quantitative and qualitative aspects of buildings through a point system or scorecard. Most of these systems assess both expected (design and planning) performance and actual (post-occupancy) performance. Although distinct from one another, all the rating systems aspire to give rise to durable, sustainable, and enjoyable structures. All rating systems have prerequisites; projects cannot get certifications if they violate a system's tenets, such as building on a protected habitat. Many of the systems can be customized on the basis of building type, size, and location.

Let's take a brief look at a few rating systems. LEED focuses on the built environment's impact on human health and wellness. The system has several categories and point systems. In the Building Design + Construction system, points are available for integrative process, location and transportation, sustainable sites, water efficiency, energy and atmosphere, materials and resources, indoor environmental quality, innovation in design, and regional priority.

These categories are distinct from the ones for Core + Shell or Operations + Maintenance systems.

WELL also focuses on the built environment's impact on human health and wellness. Both it and LEED offer professional accreditation as well as building certification. Designers can take exams and pursue continuing education to earn credentials.

The Living Building Challenge, perhaps the most ambitious and strict rating system, focuses on high-level performance in seven categories: place, water, energy, health + happiness, materials, equity, and beauty. The Living Building Challenge recognizes buildings that improve social and economic, not just environmental, aspects of their sites and communities.

Even if a material comes from nature, architects need to fully assess whether the material is actually good for the environment or sustainable buildings. Some of the questions they ask include the following:

- How was the material harvested? Was another plant put in its place? How many years does it take for the plant to regenerate?

- How far did the material travel to get to the site?

- What does it take to maintain the material or system?

- How can we change or fix the material, when needed, and what happens when it leaves the building site?

Some so-called green materials are not actually good for the environment. For example, some building materials use recycled elements like plastic bottles and wood chips, but when these elements are assembled into new composite materials, they make material systems that do not easily break down. Once that so-called recycled material is at the end of its life cycle, it will simply sit in a landfill for decades, even centuries, until innovators discover new ways to break down and reuse it.

LOOKING AHEAD

By 2035, it is estimated, 75 percent of the built environment will be new or renovated. Architects have a lot of exciting work ahead. In addition to designing new structures with higher standards for environmental performance at lower costs, and with more benefits for occupants and communities, architects will be working on energy audits to study how existing structures can be adapted. Their work will incorporate structural retrofitting and features for energy optimization and efficient water use. Ideally, architects will be able to work with project partners to make structures and entire cities that are self-sustaining.

Architects will not only be looking at large-scale systems and ways of changing how we interact with buildings; they will also be studying the small-scale aspects of design, such as long-lasting and low-energy-use products like specialized light bulbs and thermal glazing. The energy use of fixtures can be reduced with sensors, timers, and motion detectors. Inhabitants can further reduce energy consumption by manipulating other fixtures—for example, by adjusting shades to block unnecessary light and reduce cooling loads.

Environmentally conscious buildings usually have recycling plans for waste and areas for collection of recyclable materials by type (paper, plastic, glass, compostable matter), and they may use composting for gardening. Rainwater may be captured and collected for irrigation, and greywater from noncontaminated sources in the building, such as toilet flushing, may be put to use. One of the most exciting aspects of sustainable architecture is that buildings will generate power, foster ecosystems, and give rise to stronger, more interconnected communities.

FORWARD-THINKING SOLUTIONS

Architects have to think outside the box to tackle climate change, handle population growth, and make more robust and equitable communities that address ambitious approaches to sustainability, such as the United Nation's Global Goals. Some exhilarating projects explore demountable buildings that can move around the world to reduce the footprint associated with temporary structures that need to be erected for global events, such as the Olympics or the World Cup. Architects are exploring biophilic design, which fully assesses the impact nature has on humans and how buildings need to be inextricably connected to the natural world for the health and happiness of the inhabitants. These buildings are pushing the boundaries between what is inside and outside, as well as what a living building can look like.

As temperatures and sea levels rise across the globe, it's clear that architects need to work on long-term solutions to sustainable building as well as bold proposals that can make immediate impacts. Gray Organschi Architecture is interested in expanding the use of wood in contemporary construction projects, from small-scale residences to even skyscrapers. Instead of relying on steel and concrete, both of which have a huge environmental footprint, a city of tall wooden buildings could actually become a living carbon sink. This architectural urban forest could clean the air while providing intriguing places for people to live and work.

Pushing this idea of productive architecture further, the design firm Farming Architects is asking some innovative questions, such as: What if our civic buildings, schools, and restaurants could have living walls to grow vegetables through hydroponics (soilless plant growth) and collect rainwater-fueled aquaponics to raise fish? We could create a whole meal from a building—with zero waste!

Architects are also exploring design beyond the terrestrial realm. Some are pondering underwater architecture and whole cities beneath the seas, while others are testing ideas for designing and building on other planets. What would architecture on Mars—a planet that has intense radiation, low oxygen levels, and destructive dust storms—look like? A standard house certainly wouldn't work, and how would we even get materials to the site?

These types of projects question the limits of our imagination and the capacities for building in unexplored territories. Radical ideas and questions are necessary in architecture to drive the profession forward. Architect Sir Norman Foster said, "As an architect, you design for the present, with an awareness of the past, for a future which is essentially unknown."

Chapter 3
HOW ARCHITECTS SHAPE SPACES

THE WORK OF AN ARCHITECT can go far beyond the realm of buildings. Architects and collaborative teams of designers, engineers, and builders create the structures that connect our world and provide places for recreation and play, including bridges, ports, and open places for gathering. If we think about a few famous cities around the world, some of the most recognized and celebrated places are actually open spaces, rather than buildings. Cities such as London, Paris, and Rome are noted for their public paths, plazas (also known as squares or piazzas), and parks.

The character of these public spaces often changes over the course of a day or season. For example, a public plaza can be a place of transience during the day, with people moving to and from work or errands. But it can take on a totally different feel at night, becoming a dynamic and vibrant place for locals and visitors to meet and socialize. These spaces can be sites of collective, peaceful assembly one day, calling governments or other organizations into action, and animated urban theaters or festival sites on another day.

Public spaces can also be marketplaces for selling goods, food, or drink, allowing residents to access economic opportunity through small business ventures and cities to offer fresh, local food options to their residents. Food deserts—areas where it's hard to find fresh food or access grocery stores via pedestrian access or public transportation—are prevalent in the underserved areas of cities. Public markets provide options for healthy lifestyles, and they support local farmers and businesses.

Throughout history, we can find countless examples of extraordinary architecture that was built for private use, including castles, palaces, certain religious structures, offices, and other residential building types. These structures, however, are reserved for select people. Public architecture makes examples of thoughtful and well-executed design accessible to everyone.

Outdoor public spaces provide flexibility in their use. Although they are more subject to the elements, such as rain and wind, they can evolve over time and are typically essential to the character of a particular city or culture. For example, North America's first public park was Boston Common in Massachusetts. Today we may think of parks primarily as places to play soccer, have a picnic, or sunbathe, but from its foundation in 1634 until the early 1800s, Boston Common was a place where local residents could take their livestock to graze.

In Savannah, Georgia, North America's first planned city (c.1733), General James Oglethorpe was a pioneering urban designer who proposed a gridded plan with 24 interspersed public squares. Nearly 300 years later, those squares are still treasured, shaded places to read a book or sketch the incredible architecture of the city beneath towering live oak trees. Even though they were organized before the use of automobiles, Savannah's squares also help make the city more pedestrian friendly because cars need to substantially slow down to navigate the streets around the squares.

Public parks are often called the "lungs of a city" because they provide access to fresh air and spaces to exercise as well as enjoy nature, benefiting mental and physical health. As noted in the last chapter, recent studies in biophilic design prove that humans are happier and healthier when they feel connected to nature.

This chapter explores how architects think about public spaces and work with various stakeholders to innovate in communities with different needs.

DEEP DIVE

The city of San Francisco is famous for its architecture and the iconic Golden Gate Bridge (1937), as well as breathtaking views across the bay on days when the notorious fog clears. The fog, which is caused by variable temperatures mixing with different wind patterns and ocean currents, is a visual cue that there are a lot of competing environmental factors and forces in this coastal city. As an additional complication, the city is within one of the nation's most hazardous seismic zones, so it is

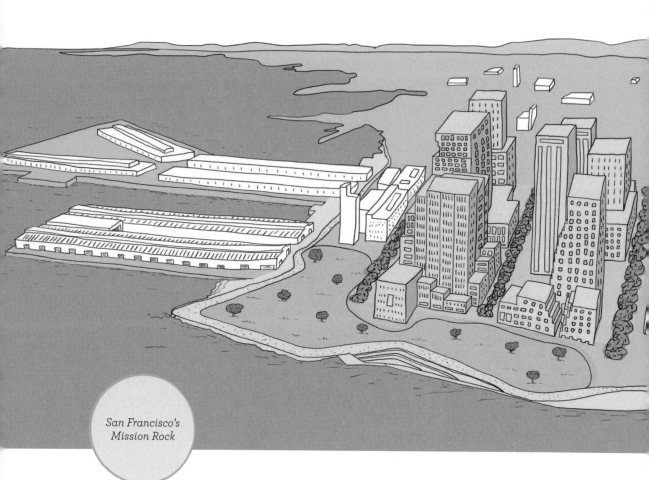

*San Francisco's
Mission Rock*

susceptible to not only earthquakes but also resulting landslides and soil liquification. With so many challenges, San Francisco may appear to be a frustrating or even futile place for design innovation. But architects truly excel in this situation, as they are able to approach complex sites and intersecting issues with enthusiasm and optimism.

Mission Rock is a new 28-acre master plan for development along the waterfront of McCovey Cove and the San Francisco Bay. A number of different architectural firms (including Henning Larsen, MVRDV, Studio Gang, and WORKac) are developing strategies to protect the city against rising sea levels. The project will also rehabilitate the historic Pier 48, a former industrial site that has been converted to an open-air event space, and link the area to public transportation and roadways. With such an intricate site and ambitious goals, collaboration is key!

Landscape architects from SCAPE, Miller Company, and Min Design proposed an expansive design for a green space near Pier 48, known as China Basin Park. This waterfront promenade and open park will be a place for rest and recreation, with bike paths, tiered steps into the bay, and kayak launches. The site is across from the Giants' baseball stadium, so visitors will be able to watch games from the built-in waterfront benches and even from boats in the cove.

The park will also incorporate a system for reviving the area's compromised intertidal ecosystems, so people can engage in healthy exercise while improving the health of the surrounding environment. Native plants will encourage an active habitat along a constructed wetland, attracting birds and other forms of wildlife. In addition to the expansive green areas of the park and the Great Lawn near Pier 48, the project will have a series of smaller pocket parks where groups can gather and play. A Blue Greenway will connect the wetland to pedestrian and cycling paths throughout the city.

The master plan consists of varied open spaces as well as a mixed-use neighborhood where locals and visitors will be able to enjoy amenities like shopping, dining, concert venues, and public art installations. Office space will be convenient for those living on the site, with 40 percent of the residences allocated as affordable housing. This aspect is extremely important because San Francisco's real estate prices are particularly high. Mission Rock aims to be an equitable and diverse neighborhood, with environmental and economic resilience at the core of its identity.

WHAT ARCHITECTS CAN DO

Architects do far more than design structures. They can also help envision the way entire communities live, work, learn, play, remember, and keep healthy. Let's take a look at how they do it.

Shape Communities for Smart Growth

Architects can help design places that are safe and healthy, where residents can easily access school and work, as well as grocery stores, shops, community facilities, and places for recreation. They can plan for smart growth so there is room for population increase. Imagine living in a community where you could reach everything you need by walking, biking, or taking public transportation. This type of holistic design is characteristic of the so-called New Urbanist community, a great example of which can be found in Seaside, Florida.

Designed by Andrés Duany and Elizabeth Plater-Zyberk, Seaside is a walkable town that brought a number of architects together to create an idealized layout. The paths, views, and scale of the structures are focused on pedestrians, not cars. The landscape architecture and details applied to the homes, civic buildings, and public spaces are unique and carefully constructed to respond to the climate. Within this beach community, it's easy to find a shady place to read a book or sit and talk with a neighbor. Good architecture inspires us to take moments of pause and truly study our surroundings.

In such places, community members collaborate with architects to create strong neighborhoods that are dense and well connected. Farmlands, wetlands, and other types of habitat preserves are left untouched, so the built and natural environments are complementary.

Design Memorials

Landscape architects and architects are often responsible for creating spaces of commemoration and remembrance, such as cemeteries and memorials. As somber but essential spaces, these designs can help bring a sense of peace and relief to grieving family members and friends, while also serving as visual markers for different people, places, and ideas within history.

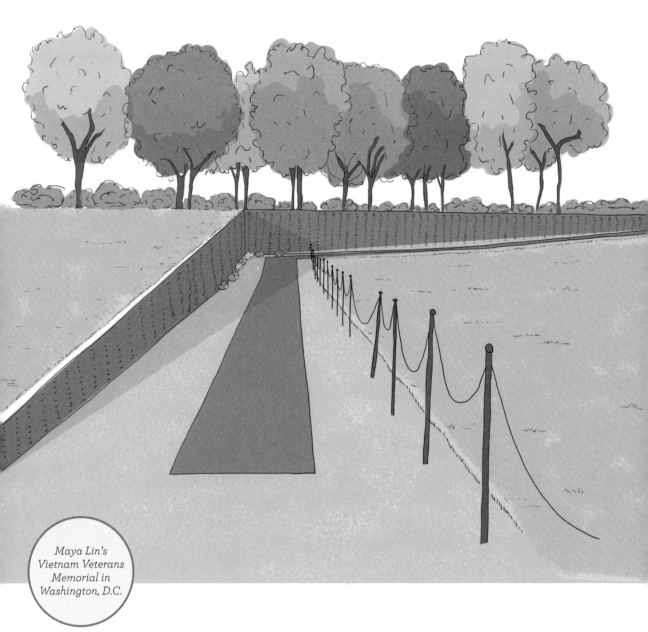

Maya Lin's
Vietnam Veterans
Memorial in
Washington, D.C.

Architectural designer and artist Maya Lin is well known for her
memorials, and she won the competition for the Vietnam Veterans Memorial in Washington, D.C., when she was a 21-year-old architecture student.
In the decades since then, she has completed the Civil Rights Memorial
in Montgomery, Alabama; the Women's Table at her alma mater, Yale

University; and many other projects that are integral to bringing the stories and emotions of history to life.

There are a number of notable architect-designed memorials around the world, from the famous Great War monuments in northern France to all the commemorative landscapes in Washington, D.C. Some of these places are dedicated to certain people or events, but others focus on telling the story of a particular time and difficult histories that have been previously overlooked.

For example, at the University of Virginia, the Memorial to Enslaved Laborers celebrates those who helped construct the famous landmarks of the Rotunda and the Academical Village and who were forced into service for students and faculty. As a memorial, it pays careful attention to the use of materials so the form's color and texture vary under different weather and light conditions. It is a place for reflection, but also for education and community gatherings.

Rethink How We Harvest Food

Following their success in an international design competition, a team of architecture students from the University of California, Berkeley, and their professors collaborated with the internationally renowned Tokyo-based design firm Kengo Kuma and Associates. The competition challenged students to propose environmentally friendly designs for a garden, and the team came up with a plan for growing, harvesting, and eating food on site. It even included a system for composting waste back into the garden as natural fertilizer. During the cold winter months, the site can serve as a greenhouse. It uses local materials and building techniques to respond to traditional architecture of the region while visually calling attention to a new way of farming and celebrating the important act of sharing a meal within a community.

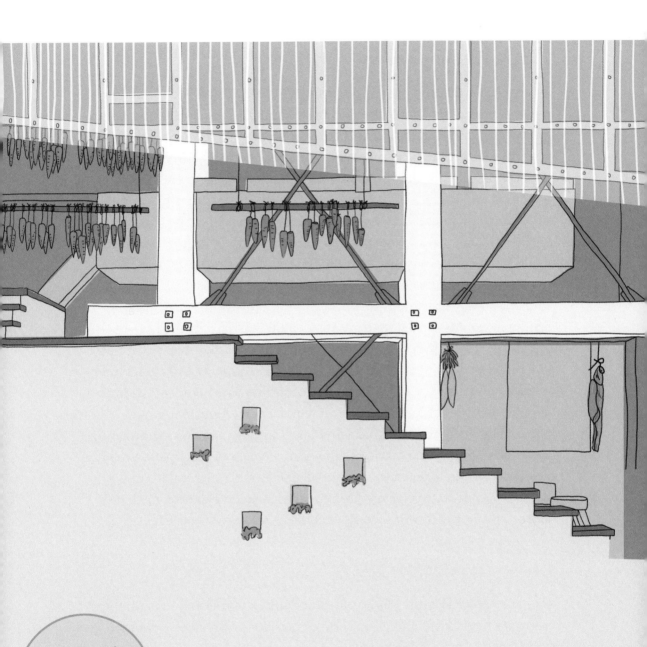

Nest We Grow by
UC Berkekey College
of Environmental Design
with Kengo Kuma and
Associates, in
Hokkaido, Japan

Shape Places for Play

Do you have a favorite park or playground? What makes that space unique? Students at Auburn University's School of Architecture, Landscape Architecture, and Planning in Alabama can participate in a residential program called the Rural Studio. Founded by Samuel Mockbee and D. K. Ruth in 1993, the program gives students an opportunity to design and build new structures and spaces for their neighbors in Hale County. This area is plagued with poverty, so the students take the role of citizen architects who help build a better community. About 1,000 students have completed nearly 270 projects through the Rural Studio. These projects range from houses to community centers and amenities for parks, such as Marion, Alabama's Perry Lakes Park Pavilion and Birding Tower, which allow visitors to experience nature from a very unique perspective. These places are designed for different users and age groups, and they inspire the next generation of designers to make incredible spaces for children to let their imaginations run wild. Over the course of several years, students designed and built installations at Lions Park in Greensboro, Alabama, to enrich the park and diversify the available activities. The park includes a shade structure to keep people cool during their walks, a concrete skate park, a mobile concession stand to use during baseball games and other events, and a massive play space constructed from reused 55-gallon oil drums, where echoes of laughter reverberate against the galvanized surfaces.

Create an Urban Oasis

We have explored some public parks and urban plazas, but most of these examples have been open to the sky, or perhaps just shaded by some well-placed trees. What happens in hotter climates, where people need to escape the heat and direct sunlight? In Seville, Spain, the Metropol Parasol by the architectural firm J. MAYER H. uses a lofted canopy that spans a large portion of the plaza to create a shady space for pedestrians, as well as nearby restaurants and a farmers' market. Portions of

the structure are elevated in order to provide different views across the cityscape and capture breezes that would be otherwise blocked by the surrounding buildings. The variations in the ground levels, complete with built-in seating and planters, also make it a great place to watch Seville's skateboarders.

This structure is one of the largest ever made from timber, and the mushroom-shaped pieces fit together like a massive 3D puzzle to create a shading lattice. The Metropol Parasol isn't made from monolithic (big) timber pieces from individual trees but instead from smaller pieces of wood that were laminated together. The resulting environmental footprint of the project is smaller because it didn't require old-growth trees. The construction process was also more efficient because pieces could be fabricated off-site and then transported to be assembled within the plaza.

Make Safer Habitats

Architects, landscape architects, engineers, other product designers, and biologists are collaborating to create animal architecture. This ecologically responsive design can take many forms, including green bridges, atypical culverts, roadside berms, antireflective coatings or patterns on windows, and even elements on buildings that encourage birds to nest or pollinators such as bees to flourish. These pieces of critical infrastructure are placed along major roads, highways, and developments to foster safer wildlife corridors. The designs ensure that mammals, amphibians, and birds can complete their migration cycles and quests for food without becoming roadkill or, in the case of birds, casualties of highly reflective buildings that distort their perception of sky and surface. These designs envision how the built and natural worlds can coexist.

Develop Master Plans

Beyond the scale of a single building or bounded urban area around a public square, architects work on large-scale master plans that rethink whole neighborhoods and sections of cities. These mixed-use projects incorporate a range of building types, such as residences, businesses, offices, schools, and other places dedicated to public use and green space.

These master plans also consider transportation infrastructure, addressing questions like: How do people move within the neighborhood—ideally through walking, biking, or public transportation? Do those transit points connect to a larger system that allows people to move across the city, like a bus or train system, or transportation that accesses other cities and towns, like interstate buses, trains, and planes? How do personal cars fit into the system?

Habitat bridge

Sadly, these plans are sometimes paper projects, meaning they are never built. But this kind of design exercise is still valuable because it creates relationships within communities, questions the resilience of places, and imagines aspects of redevelopment that can be implemented in phases as funds and support become available. Whether built or imagined, master plan projects can be catalysts for beneficial change and encourage reinvestment in places that are underused or underserved.

CAREERS IN ARCHITECTURE

As you are discovering, architecture is a varied and collaborative profession. This section looks at a few related disciplines that are particularly instrumental to the practice of architecture when it comes to the creation of large-scale projects for public use.

Landscape Architects

Although landscape architecture is a relatively new profession, designed manipulations of the landscape have existed for millennia, including the Hanging Gardens of Babylon, one of the Seven Ancient Wonders of the World.

But landscape architects do much more than design gardens. They study aesthetics and science across natural systems, hydrology, geology, plants, topography, soils, climate, and ecology. With this knowledge, they design and implement projects that are beneficial to both the built and natural environments. Their designs can be composed of entirely new constructions, but their projects can also deal with conservation, remediation, restoration, and rehabilitation.

Landscape architecture is a growing field, especially as we become more and more attuned to sustainable approaches to the built environment. These designs deal with water and stormwater management, as well as the cultivation of active lifestyles via playgrounds, parks, and public sport complexes. Thanks to the work of landscape architects, we have walking, hiking, and biking trails, and we can stroll beneath the shade of well-selected trees, rest on thoughtfully placed benches, and use other types of street furniture, such as bike racks.

Frederick Law Olmsted (1822–1903) is known as the father of American landscape architecture. His most famous work is Central Park in New York City, which carefully considered the landscape as a part of its design. Along with ten other members, Olmsted founded the American Society of

Landscape Architects (ASLA) in 1899. Today, landscape and urban design studios like SCAPE are tackling some of the greatest design challenges of the 21st century by rethinking waterfronts to survive sea-level rise, reviving and expanding compromised ecosystems, and creating public parks. Through the work of landscape architects, we can all benefit from healthier and happier communities.

Urban Planners

Buildings are just one part of a working city. There are also pieces of transportation infrastructure like roads, railways, and vehicles. We have street furniture such as lampposts and benches, and various bits of elevated wiring and urban vegetation. We also have myriad systems buried beneath the ground such as subways and sewers. These pieces of a city are like gears within a larger system, and this mechanism is further complicated by all its users.

The city must accommodate pedestrians, cyclists, drivers, and public transport commuters, some of whom know the city well and others who are trying to navigate it for the first time. Urban planners, also sometimes known as city and regional planners or urban designers, study and design for all these systems and users. They help activate the relationships between the built environment, the community, and governmental entities with policies such as zoning, or rules governing what can be built where.

Just like buildings, urban-planning solutions are varied. Urban planners have to consider present-day operations and the local climate, but their designs also evaluate how a city will function and change in 5, 10, or 50 years. They can have different specialties in sustainable growth or real estate development, and, like so many with careers related to architecture, urban planners can also have interdisciplinary expertise, combining two fields of study. Common intersections are human health, law, and business.

Civil Engineers

Like architecture, engineering requires specialized education, work experience, and the completion of a series of examinations. Certain civil engineers focus on how a building is physically made. They deal with special tools, structural supporting systems, and infrastructure needed to bring construction materials and machinery to the site. They also address how these items will be removed once a building is completed and how the structure will undergo any large-scale maintenance.

A few other veins of the engineering discipline work directly with architects. For example, architectural engineers and structural engineers are both specialist fields that straddle architecture and civil engineering. These fields use engineering principles and building technology to innovate solutions to project-based questions. For example, they assess how buildings can have a physically lighter impact on the environment, examine options for structural supports that do not compromise the aesthetics or overall concept of a building, and determine how a building can redirect natural light and wind in a city so it doesn't create a heat island or a wind tunnel.

LOOKING AHEAD

In the coming years, expect increases in both urban populations and urban density. Projects are exploring how people can live in closer proximity to work and other services, with more shared resources and vital public space. This means avoiding sprawl, protecting undeveloped land and waterfronts, and creating an important balance between the built and natural worlds. With these ambitions in mind, large-scale adaptive reuse projects will be some of the most important undertakings for architecture, landscape architects, engineers, developers, and community stakeholders.

As noted earlier, many large abandoned sites that are good candidates for developments are brownfields. Without mitigation, they propose threats to human health as contaminants leach into the ground and waterways. But when treated properly, these sites can become stunning examples of creative reinvention. For example, designers are tackling adaptive-reuse projects at the decommissioned steel mills of Pittsburgh and the surrounding area, the shuttered automobile manufacturing plants along areas of the Rust Belt such as Detroit, and the abandoned textile mills in the American South, in places like Raleigh-Durham, North Carolina.

Large manufacturing sites are prime locations for redevelopment and reinvestment. Because of their size, they are relatively flexible for different uses, from residential and retail complexes to corporate headquarters and cultural centers such as museums and concert venues. In fact, some of the most successful adaptive reuse projects combined all these programs together to create great places where different ages and groups of people can comingle. Sites with mixed uses are also vibrant during both the day and evening hours, making them safer and more welcoming.

One of the most famous brownfield redevelopment projects in the world is the High Line in New York City, a 1.5-mile elevated railway that was integral to the Meatpacking District in Chelsea in the 1900s. The trains ceased operations in the 1980s, and the railway sat abandoned for more than two decades before a team of community activists, designers, and ecologists came together to reimagine the site as a linear urban park. It is now one of the most popular destinations in the city, and it spurred a series of adjacent redevelopment projects.

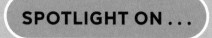

SPOTLIGHT ON . . .

VALERIE S. FRIEDMANN

URBAN PLANNER FOR THE CITY OF LEXINGTON, KENTUCKY, DIVISION OF PLANNING

What does a typical workday look like?
I spend most days dividing my energy between three categories of work, which are distinct but very related. First and foremost, working for local government means I am a public servant, so a large portion of my time is spent engaging with our community. Next, I spend time coordinating with other government divisions to make sure that the community's vision and goals for open space and green space are being met as our city continues to grow. And finally, I spend time working with the development community by reviewing their upcoming projects to make sure they also support our goals. Making connections and balancing with all these different groups is something that my design education really prepared me to do.

Why did you want to be a designer/landscape architect?
When I was a kid, my favorite books were vintage field guides. I could spend hours learning about the world in my backyard, especially the plants. I was fascinated by those books, not only for their information, but also for their beautiful drawings and maps. At the same time, I have always loved observing the way people use spaces and reflecting on what makes a space feel more like a place. I became a landscape architect because of this enchantment with green-growing things, the beauty of leaves, flowers, and maps, and a desire to create places where people feel happy, welcome, and appreciated—all while being surrounded by the beauty of plants.

Where did you go to school?

I have a Bachelor of Science in Landscape Design and Construction as well as a Master of Landscape Architecture from the University of Tennessee, Knoxville.

What has been the most challenging part about your job?

As a designer, I spend a lot of time visiting and learning about places that do a great job of addressing the needs of people and the environment. Being familiar with those great examples means I can get overwhelmed by all the not-so-good design that's out there.

What's your favorite/the most rewarding part about your job?

The flipside to what's most challenging for me is what's most rewarding—knowing I can help make the world a better place with design.

What advice would you give to someone who's thinking about becoming a designer?

Learn early how to listen to people when they tell you what their community needs—don't just hear what you want to hear. The same goes for the landscape.

AT ONE POINT IN AMERICA'S HISTORY, mill towns flourished. Nestled along the natural falls, these towns formed sinuous river communities that were particularly active from the 1820s through the 1980s. The entrepreneurialism and productivity of textile manufacturing in America shaped a way of life. Through commercial investment in community endeavors, the towns were constructed around innovative mixed-use plans with vibrant main-street economies and architecturally distinctive private and public structures, from schools to gymnasiums to theaters. The closure of the mills and shift toward overseas production, however, rapidly changed the demographics and architectural landscape of these areas. Many of the large-scale mills were demolished, and some were dismantled for architectural salvage. There was a mass exodus of community members because of high unemployment rates, and many of these mill towns are now entirely bypassed.

But some innovative designers, investors, and community members are helping revive mill towns across the United States. The Hamilton Canal Innovation District Plan in Lowell, Massachusetts, is working to revive an underused area and transform it into a new gateway for the city and a place for new residents and visitors to explore a historic canal and fabrication center. Factory spaces were converted into artist studios and apartments, many of which are affordable to most residents, while the mill yards became parks. The powerhouses that once ran the mill now support the regional power grid. The interconnectivity of the mill also made it a perfect place to expand public transportation through bridges, trolley lines, and paths for both pedestrians and bikes. The area is now known as transit-oriented and a model for smart-growth development.

Mill revitalization projects are just one example of how architects work with communities to revive historic places and give them new life as models of sustainability. The projects use reclaimed materials, employ energy- and water-efficient fixtures, use alternatives to fossil fuels, encourage activity through recreational and social spaces, and foster green spaces in reimagined parks and on rooftops. These types of projects are happening around the country, from Milwaukee, Wisconsin, and Detroit, Michigan, to Durham and Greensboro in North Carolina, with each community discovering that abandoned spaces can be entirely revived with some creativity.

Sustainable Lowell 2025 canal redevelopment

DEEP DIVE

So far, we have primarily explored how architects can enact change through their design practice, whether at the scale of an individual building or a large urban plan, so their architectural products can be conduits for sustainable communities. But what about the process of architectural design? How can we ensure that all the necessary voices are heard during the development, design, and planning phases of a project? What happens when architects and their clients don't work with the community where their project will be located?

A thoughtful, collaborative approach to smart design and community growth involves a number of different perspectives. This is where community design centers excel. Their staff work with different design professionals, clients, businesses, governmental agencies, policymakers, and, most important, local communities to examine and tackle design and planning challenges with the public interest at the heart of all decisions.

Several community design centers are managed by, or in partnership with, schools of architecture. This means architecture students have the opportunity to work on real-world local projects during their design education and these experiences provide the essential foundations for cultivating citizen architects who will pursue careers grounded in public service design. By bringing creative designers, makers, funders, and engaged community members together to share and shape project goals, community design centers foster better and more interconnected cities.

Founded the same year that Hurricane Katrina crippled the city, the Albert and Tina Small Center for Collaborative Design at the Tulane School of Architecture works within New Orleans, Louisiana. The center brings together architects, developers, specialty organizations, and the general public to create comprehensive and integrated design solutions.

Rather than serving as a full-service design studio, this space is a catalyst to connect community members with the design professionals and stakeholders who are completing projects in the city. This connection ensures that projects are better aligned with the needs and vision of the local community, not just the ambitions of an outside company that may lack some fundamental understandings about the area, its history, and the unique challenges that the community may face.

These programs expand access to the design process and empower young students to be leaders in their communities to seek positive change. The Small Center for Collaborative Design has completed more than 80 projects and involved more than 2,000 people in the collaborative design process to create food stores and community gardens, wetland conservation and learning centers, early education environments, pavilions, homeless day centers and transitional housing projects, and smart transportation solutions. Many of these projects were design/build, meaning the project teams worked together from the planning phases all the way through construction and initial operation.

Although this design center and others like it are intently focused on their local community, they ensure their work is transparent and well documented through websites, public meetings, and publications. They openly and broadly share the successes and challenges of specific projects so the work within one community can serve as a beneficial model for others. If you want to learn more about the diverse work of community design centers around the nation, the Association of Collegiate Schools of Architecture (ACSA) and the Association for Community Design maintain lists of active community design centers.

Environmental Sustainability

As we explored in the last chapter, the disposability of buildings in the modern age is a substantial concern for architects and builders. If we look into the record of architectural history, earlier civilizations built for centuries, or even millennia, but many buildings from the 20th and 21st centuries had short life spans of just 40 or so years. Given the materials

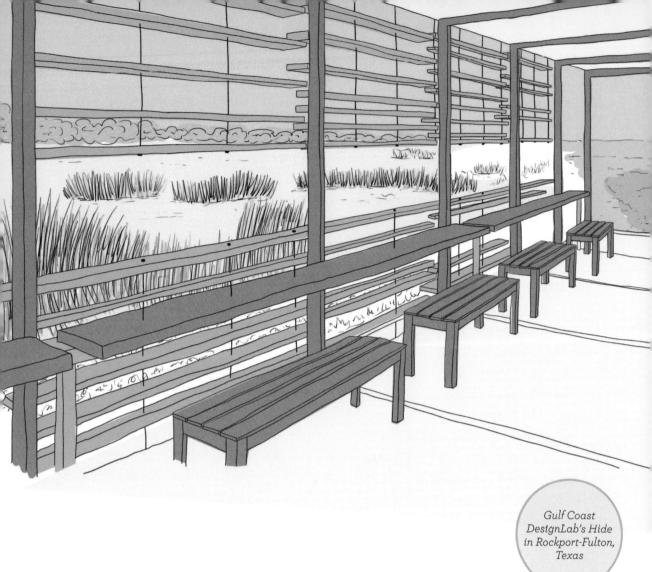

and labor needed to construct and disassemble them, those buildings left a
very poor and resource-dependent environmental footprint.

We also have to question what happened to those materials. Were
they broken down and responsibly recycled or reused, or were they simply
moved to a garbage dump? In the latter case, many of those materials will
take a substantial amount of time to break down. In the worst-case sce-
nario, a building's materials could take more time to decompose than the
building was actually in use.

So how do we ensure longevity and smaller environmental footprints for our buildings? First, it is important to assess the cost of a building with a bigger picture in mind—not just the initial costs of design and construction, but also what it would take to modify or decommission (to withdraw from use) the building.

With this full life cycle in mind, stakeholders may be willing to invest more in a building from the beginning phases to ensure that it is adaptable to changes in use or operations in the future. Clients and communities also need to see the value in renovating and retrofitting existing structures, rather than championing entirely new buildings.

Another architectural concept that can help ensure that projects are environmentally sustainable is the idea that buildings should touch the earth lightly. This phrase has roots in the work of Australian architect Glenn Murcutt. Unlike many other famous contemporary architects, he works exclusively in Australia and has refined his designs through a professional practice that pays astute attention to the local and natural conditions of a site: its climate, soil, topography, vegetation, and history.

Architectural critics describe Murcutt's work as sensitive to the land and surrounding communities, such as taking cues from aboriginal architecture to shape the form, materiality, and spatial layers of his projects. His work also makes extensive use of natural light and passive systems, moving away from a modern reliance on electricity and air-conditioning. Murcutt makes spaces that are useable and pleasant to occupy without the need for extensive energy consumption. For Murcutt, a project is successful if it emulates the qualities and tranquility of sitting beneath a tree; architecture should not be a sealed box that divorces the inhabitant from the elements.

Operating with similar premises, the Gulf Coast DesignLab of the University of Texas's School of Architecture is a design/build studio that creates environmental education and recreation projects. These projects are intended to enhance the landscape through subtle and responsive built interventions. The studio's constructed bird observatories and outdoor classrooms actually become part of the area's ecosystem.

Diversity, Equity, and Inclusion

To beneficially impact diversity, equity, and inclusion, architects need to design for whole communities, not just the clients paying the bills. There will always be important private commissions, but citizen architects will consider how their structures will create places for inclusion, not exclusion. They will also strive to thoughtfully design each commission, whether it is a school in a low-income community or a library at a private university.

It may be uncomfortable to think about, but architects are involved in the design and construction of spaces such as prisons and other correctional facilities. They consider how these structures can be safe, secure, and humane not only for the people who work there, but also for those who are incarcerated. Architectural commissions have to cover a broad range of building typologies, and design should not be reserved for those with privilege of place or finances.

Equitable and affordable housing is one of the biggest challenges for architecture in the modern age. As we see rental prices soar in cities, how can we ensure that urban areas are not entirely gentrified and that all levels of income can find housing that is comfortable and reliable? The documentary *The Pruitt-Igoe Myth* (2011) tells the story of public subsidized housing and how a 33-building complex in St. Louis, Missouri, completed in 1954, transformed from an icon of urban development to a cautionary tale of depravity and violence in only 20 years.

The trials of public housing continue today, as seen by the Grenfell Tower disaster in London in 2017, where a public housing project with a defective building skin made the structure extremely susceptible to fire. As we look toward development in the 21st century, it will be essential for architects to address the need for safe, affordable housing for all while also ensuring that those structures, and the surrounding public spaces, carefully address accessibility and the needs of aging populations.

Beyond making built environments that encourage and sustain diversity, equity, and inclusion, the architectural profession has to do some work to address representation in the field, including improving paths to architectural education and practice for a broad range of students and aspiring designers.

Although more than half of the architecture students around the United States are female, only about 30 percent of licensed architects are women. In general, there is a lack of role models in both academic and professional spheres of architecture, especially for women and people of color. How can we make a more diverse profession when younger students do not know architecture is a feasible career option for them?

Let's look at how both the academy and the profession are working to become more inclusive and accessible:

- Local AIA chapters and other companies have developed mentorship and outreach programs to allow high school and college students to shadow an architect or visit construction sites on a regular basis in order to better understand the profession and its products.

- First- and second-generation college students might see architecture as a major where the return on investment may take too long. As a career, architecture requires a significant investment in both education and time before you are licensed and established in the profession. More industry-funded scholarships are available for underrepresented groups in the profession and certain schools are working to reduce the cost of supplies for architecture school.

- To address the lack of accessibility and equity within professional practice, firms are exploring how their operations can shift to accommodate better work-life balances, especially for those with families and other personal obligations. This includes working remotely, job shares, and flexibility of working hours.

Physical and Mental Well-Being

Can successful architecture make us happier and healthier? We certainly know that buildings with functional errors, poor materials, and bad ventilation can cause health problems. In *The Architecture of Happiness* (2006), Alain de Botton explores how buildings can make us feel exposed and self-conscious or relaxed and inspired. The idea of beauty, and what makes a particular building beautiful, has changed over time and can vary across cultures. Is beauty found in the peacefulness and simplicity of a project or in the exercise of experimental design?

Perhaps one of the best ways for us to explore how architecture can enhance physical and mental well-being is to explore places like hospitals and treatment centers. These spaces, which cater to those seeking rest and relief, should accommodate the same levels of comfort and design ingenuity as hospitality sites such as resorts and hotels, with ample access to light, air, and outdoor spaces.

Finnish architect Alvar Aalto realized this need when he entered a competition in 1928 for a sanatorium. The building was designed for tuberculosis patients and, having overcome a serious illness himself, Aalto realized it was critical to design from the perspective of the patient. What was the view from the bed? Was the lighting too harsh? Were the interior spaces easy to navigate and visually appealing? Could aspects of the outdoors make their way into the building? He also carefully designed and fabricated special furniture that could be easily sanitized and would be comfortable for patients who needed to be in a reclined position. Today, there is a name for Aalto's critical approach to functional and beneficial architecture: evidence-based design.

Maggie's Centers are contemporary structures that push evidence-based design even further. Co-founded by architectural critic Charles Jencks in honor of his wife, these forward-thinking cancer treatment centers fully explore the concept that buildings can uplift and actively contribute to a patient's overall health and well-being. Often described as havens, these buildings have distinct ties between the built and natural environment, linking interior and exterior spaces. They resemble collective housing units and nature retreats with distinctive landscapes more than hospitals. Famous architects such as Zaha Hadid, Frank Gehry, and Snøhetta have tackled the design of Maggie's Centers in the United Kingdom and Hong Kong.

Sparking Joy

As a profession, architecture is most concerned with three goals: health, safety, and welfare. These are serious, essential issues for the practice of architecture, but it is also important to have some levity within the profession. Architecture should make people happy and energized. Our built environments should be not only functional, but also memorable.

It is possible to make impactful, forward-thinking, and imaginative designs that never exist beyond paper or a 3D model. But just because a project isn't built doesn't mean it is inconsequential. Recognizing that drawing and writing are key outlets for architects, Blank Space is an online platform (BlankSpaceProject.com) and an "office for thought provocation" that challenges designers through idea competitions, such as Fairy Tales and Driverless Future. Its website is an incredible resource that showcases the endless possibilities of architecture.

In terms of sparking joy, architects help create playgrounds, recreational fields, and skate parks, but they also contribute to the over-the-top and otherworldly spaces that can be found in amusement parks. Here, they imagine how different structures and designed details can transport visitors to other places, such as a haunted house, a residence in space, or an enchanted world.

At theme parks such as Disney or Universal Studios, many of the kingdoms or worlds that visitors can explore are based on films. Architects, too, can contribute to the vision and set design for the realms, crafting impossible architecture that blends styles and places, or reimagining historic eras.

PAVAN IYER, RA

What do you do for work?

I am a registered architect and founder of eightvillage, a place-based design consultancy seeking to create positive change in communities. Ashtagrama (literally in Sanskrit, "eight villages") was a group of small communities in the Kolar District of Karnataka, India. In the early 16th century, some brahmins known as the Ashtagrama Iyers from Tamil Nadu migrated to Ashtagrama at the request of the existing government. They came as learned priests, Vedic scholars, and agriculturists, and they soon transformed the kingdom from a poor community into a well-educated and prosperous one. The firm, eightvillage, continues the ethos of the Ashtagrama by asking how to design a place-based ecology and bring an empathetic process to our work.

What does a typical workday look like?

I work with developers, community members, and nonprofits, making design proposals to enhance communities and expand access to design services. We bring together people and disciplines to make a better place. We do architecture, urban design, and real estate development. We also are called on to design and run different models of community engagement. For example, we did a design/ build light installation with the children who lived in the neighborhoods along Buford Highway in Atlanta. It isn't always typical architecture, but we use our architectural lens to help communities. Collaboration and communication are at the core of our process, and we are always energized to facilitate, mobilize, and catalyze projects that have an impact on people and our planet.

Why did you want to be an architect?

I wanted to make better, more inclusive places, and I wanted to help community members take a more active role in their environment. Beyond technical skills, architects can use design to generate a story or road map for the built environment and those who inhabit it.

What has been the most challenging part about being an architect?

There can be a lot of bureaucracy in community projects. So we explore how we can leverage our technical skill sets in these projects to ensure our works are viable.

What's your favorite/the most rewarding part about being an architect?

We enjoy working with communities and helping them raise their voices to shape spaces. With investment, there is real money and real capital, but about 50 percent of a project involves political capital. When we're doing a placemaking project, we have to invite the people who have the political will and ability to get projects completed. This work requires collaboration.

What advice would you give to someone who's thinking about studying architecture and/or becoming an architect?

Get to know your community and its needs. Be present; go outside your comfort zone.

We don't have to visit a dedicated playscape or theme park to see architecture that makes us laugh. For example, there are examples around the United States of roadside attractions, which architect Robert Venturi called ducks—novelty structures that humorously express their use, such as the Big Duck that sold eggs on Long Island. Other famous examples are the Coney Island Elephant, the milk bottle creamery that was transported to the Boston Children's Museum, and the Wigwam Village Motel, a roadside hotel composed of concrete teepees, which served as inspiration for Cozy Cone Model in Pixar's *Cars* (2006).

LOOKING AHEAD

Architecture has a rich history, with many buildings and ideas to explore. As we have discovered, crafting better design solutions for the future requires us to understand and learn from the past. Looking toward the future, architecture has nearly inexhaustible possibilities. We have the material and structural capabilities to create vast cities, adapt to challenging sites, and solve many of the physical and logistical challenges that puzzled previous generations of architects.

But there are still unsolved issues and questions ahead. How do we make buildings and places that push the limits of longevity and adaptability? Through new materials and systems, can our structures have self-healing properties that would make them more resilient following natural disasters or catastrophic events? How can we continue to better understand lost sites or cultures, using architecture remnants, archaeology, and digital tools to uncover the new narratives? How can we build in extreme locations on this planet, and maybe even others, while ensuring that our buildings thoughtfully respond to and even improve the surrounding environment?

Architects will continue to rethink how we see and use spaces. For example, the typical house on an urban or suburban plot will strive to be entirely self-sufficient. What if your house could harness all the energy it needed for daily tasks while also collecting, reusing, and redistributing water for all the household fixtures, from showers and baths to kitchen sinks, toilets, and greywater recycling for use in gardens that could provide a substantial amount of fresh food? Within that home's plot, there might also be an Auxiliary Dwelling Unit (ADU). Recognizing the popularity of the small house movement, these ADUs could be used as spaces for other family members or as rental properties to ensure a bit of extra income for the residents.

At the scale of cities, architects will continue to revive overlooked and even contaminated sites. In Birmingham, Alabama, Railroad Park, by landscape architect Tom Leader and the local construction firm Brasfield & Gorrie, transformed a 19-acre former industrial site into a space for rest and recreation. During typical days, the park is a popular destination for runners, bikers, and skateboarders.

Quirky playground spaces mingle with a wetland while trains pass along the elevated railways next to the park. On weekends and during special events, the park transforms into a site for outdoor concerts and art festivals; locals fondly call it "Birmingham's Living Room." The park has also served as a conduit for development in the surrounding area. In 2013, HKS Architects completed the adjacent Regions Field, home to the Birmingham Barons Double-A baseball team, and a number of restaurants, breweries, and housing complexes followed. During home games, parts of the surrounding streets close to vehicular traffic and this part of the city becomes a destination for pedestrians and impromptu celebrations.

With all the exciting opportunities ahead in architecture, it is also important to note that there may be some changes to architectural licensure that would significantly impact the profession. In the next chapter, you'll learn about the three main elements associated with becoming an architect: education, apprenticeship, and examination. There are growing movements to streamline the process, to make it easier for the profession to reach a wider audience, to retain a greater range of diversity within the profession, and to facilitate international practice.

FORWARD-THINKING SOLUTIONS

On a global scale, the United Nations Sustainable Development Goals represent a collective movement to create, build, and maintain a more equitable, responsive, and inclusive future. Although none of the 17 goals includes the word *architecture*, they are all related to elements of the built environment and involve key steps that architects and other designers can take to make a better world for all by 2030. Let's take a look at each goal, and explore how it is connected to architecture:

1. **NO POVERTY:** Access to housing, water and sanitation systems, and community resources can stop the cycle of poverty.

2. **ZERO HUNGER:** Rethink the architecture of agricultural production and decrease the commonality of food deserts in urban and rural environments.

3. **GOOD HEALTH AND WELL-BEING:** Encourage walkable cities with access to health and hygiene services.

4. **QUALITY EDUCATION:** Open schools to all genders and economic tiers, make learning environments engaging and accessible.

5. **GENDER EQUALITY:** Reduce discriminatory policies that make certain spaces unavailable to women; ensure urban and rural environments are safe for all.

6. **CLEAN WATER AND SANITATION:** Develop and deploy affordable and low-tech systems for basic water infrastructure.

7. **AFFORDABLE AND CLEAN ENERGY:** Develop and deploy affordable systems for harnessing renewable energy.

8. **DECENT WORK AND ECONOMIC GROWTH:** Ensure the places and spaces for all laborers are safe.

9. **INDUSTRY, INNOVATION, AND INFRASTRUCTURE:** Increase manufacturing spaces to better connect local and global chains of production.

10. **REDUCED INEQUALITIES:** Make design services and well-designed spaces available to all.

11. **SUSTAINABLE CITIES AND COMMUNITIES:** Design more efficiently and inclusively, realizing that buildings operate within larger, connected systems.

12. **RESPONSIBLE CONSUMPTION AND PRODUCTION:** Reduce the disposability of buildings and design for a closed-loop system within a building's life cycle.

13. **CLIMATE ACTION:** Aim to eliminate, not just reduce, greenhouse gas emissions in the production and inhabitation of buildings.

14. **LIFE BELOW WATER:** Avoid building on compromised coastal sites, wetlands, and other areas that would negatively impact biodiversity and ecosystems.

15. **LIFE ON LAND:** Use sustainable and restorative forestry practices for building construction.

16. **PEACE, JUSTICE, AND STRONG INSTITUTIONS:** Design spaces that foster human rights.

17. **PARTNERSHIPS:** Work at local, regional, national, and international levels to establish shared visions and goals.

These are ambitious but achievable goals if designers, builders, policymakers, leaders, and communities work together. As we have learned, architecture is a highly collaborative profession, and working together will be essential to future design initiatives.

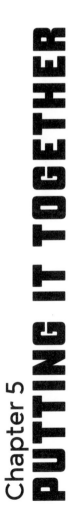

Chapter 5
PUTTING IT TOGETHER

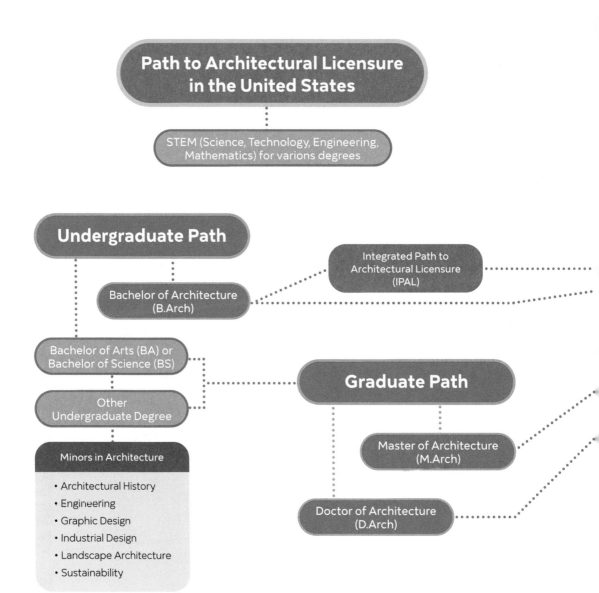

Path to Architectural Licensure in the United States

STEM (Science, Technology, Engineering, Mathematics) for various degrees

Undergraduate Path

Bachelor of Architecture (B.Arch)

Integrated Path to Architectural Licensure (IPAL)

Bachelor of Arts (BA) or Bachelor of Science (BS)

Other Undergraduate Degree

Minors in Architecture

- Architectural History
- Engineering
- Graphic Design
- Industrial Design
- Landscape Architecture
- Sustainability

Graduate Path

Master of Architecture (M.Arch)

Doctor of Architecture (D.Arch)

 National Architectural Accrediting Board (NAAB) Accredited Degree

SOME PEOPLE KNOW FROM A YOUNG AGE that they want to be architects, whereas others may arrive at the profession after pursuing different educational or career paths. There is no singular, right way to become an architect, which is one of the most fascinating aspects of the profession. Because architecture is so multifaceted, those who pursue different careers before entering that profession can bring unique perspectives to their design work.

Architectural Experience Program (AXP) completion

Architectural Registration Exams (AREs) completion

Licensure from the National Council of Architecture Registration Boards (NCARB)

Other Graduate Degrees in Design

- Master of Arts (MA) or Doctor of Philosophy (PhD) in Architectural History and Theory
- Master of Design (M.Des)
- Master of Landscape Architecture (MLA)
- Master of Science (MS) in topics such as High-Performance Building Systems, Design Technology, Design & Health, Historic Preservation and Conservation
- Master of Urban Design (MUD)
- Master of Urban and Environmental Planning
- Doctor of Design (D.Des)

Other Certifications and Examinations

- Construction Specifications Institute (CSI)
- Leadership in Energy and Environmental Design (LEED)
- National Council for Interior Design Qualification (NCIDQ) Examination
- Accredited by the International WELL Building Institute

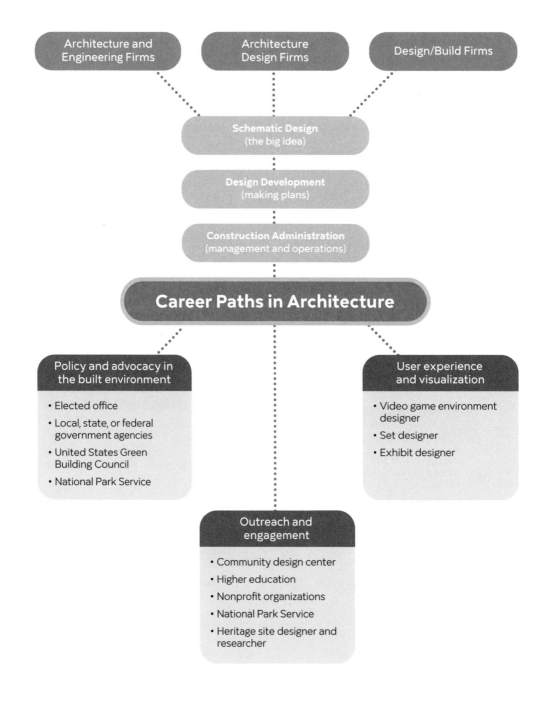

Architecture and Engineering Firms

Architecture Design Firms

Design/Build Firms

Schematic Design
(the big idea)

Design Development
(making plans)

Construction Administration
(management and operations)

Career Paths in Architecture

Policy and advocacy in the built environment

- Elected office
- Local, state, or federal government agencies
- United States Green Building Council
- National Park Service

User experience and visualization

- Video game environment designer
- Set designer
- Exhibit designer

Outreach and engagement

- Community design center
- Higher education
- Nonprofit organizations
- National Park Service
- Heritage site designer and researcher

RESOURCES

There are five main collaterals within the architecture profession, and each one represents a different facet of the path from education to practice:

AMERICAN INSTITUTE OF ARCHITECTS (AIA): The "voice of the architectural profession," the AIA was founded in 1857 to serve as an advocacy and resource group for and by architects. Beyond learning more about the national organization, you should explore your state or local AIA chapter, many of which offer a rich series of programs, both online and in person.

AMERICAN INSTITUTE OF ARCHITECT STUDENTS (AIAS): The architectural profession is unique in that students play a critical role in the profession's governance. With university-based chapters around the nation, the AIAS works to empower students and cultivate future leaders within design and service. The organization also has outreach events for younger students, and it manages Freedom By Design, a service program in partnership with National Council of Architectural Registration Boards (NCARB) that completes design/build and community-engagement projects to reduce five key barriers in the built environment: physical, educational, environmental, socioeconomic, and cultural.

ASSOCIATION OF COLLEGIATE SCHOOLS OF ARCHITECTURE (ACSA): This organization provides an educational perspective, representing architecture schools, faculty, and students around the world. All National Architectural Accrediting Board (NAAB)–accredited programs are full members, and there are also representatives from other two- and four-year schools, as well as international institutions.

NATIONAL ARCHITECTURAL ACCREDITING BOARD (NAAB): This body is responsible for evaluating academic programs in the United States and those abroad seeking Substantial Equivalency. A NAAB-accredited degree is essential to becoming a licensed architect.

NATIONAL COUNCIL OF ARCHITECTURAL REGISTRATION BOARDS (NCARB): The NCARB facilitates licensure, represents the jurisdiction for practicing architecture within the 50 states and five territories of the United States, and fosters collaboration between industry and other licensing boards across the world. They launched the Integrated Path to Architectural Licensure (IPAL) in 2015 as an additional option for aspiring architects.

One of the other main bodies within the architecture profession is the National Organization of Minority Architects (NOMA) and its student group (NOMAS). For professional organizations abroad, explore other national charters, chambers, and councils, especially the Royal Institute of British Architects (RIBA), whose site at the coveted Architecture.com site has a variety of resources.

If you are interested in learning more about architecture school and the profession, consider attending an architecture summer camp. These camps come in all different formats and lengths, both online and on campus. Some are day camps whereas others are a few weeks and they provide a glimpse of college life, including staying in residence halls. The websites for AIAS, AIA, and ACSA all maintain updated lists of architecture summer camps. The ArchCareers website also has a summer program database.

There are a variety of online resources to help expand your knowledge about the past, present, and future of architectural design:

- Read about cutting-edge design and research on ArchDaily, Architect Magazine, Dezeen, Houzz, Metropolis Magazine, Places Journal, and Uncube Magazine. Life of an Architect is also a fun blog.

- Listen to stories about creativity and interesting career paths on Design Matters, an award-winning podcast about design founded by Debbie Millman.

- Founded by architectural designer Mike Ford, HipHop Architecture introduces architecture, urban planning, and design to typically underrepresented groups within those fields. The website hosts talks and competitions and facilitates a series of exciting summer camps.

- The Institute of Classical Architecture & Art (ICAA) offers a wide range of free programs online. ICAA hosts events and chapters around the nation.

- Take a tour of North American architecture through the free database provided by the Society of Architectural Historians (SAH), called the SAH Archipedia.

- Explore the "Design" topic on TED.com for a broad collection of talks focused on architecture, urban planning, and sustainable design. You can explore other, more specific topics, too.

- The UNESCO World Heritage List recognizes natural and cultural heritage sites around the world with "universal significance."

In the digital age, architects rely on different types of design and visualization software. Many of these programs are available for free or have substantial educational discounts:

- Autodesk is a leader in computer-aided design and manufacture (CAD/CAM) software. Their educational division offers a range of programs that are free for students with a valid academic email address.

- Blender 3D Architect is a free digital-modeling platform for both Mac and PC; it is particularly good for experimentations with rendering, and it has a great online community for tutorials and tips.

- SketchUp is a user-friendly piece of digital-modeling software. There are a free web-based version and local machine-based versions that can be purchased with an educational subscription. You may have access to SketchUp for Schools through Google Apps for Education or Microsoft Education platforms. For those who want to push their modeling further, look into free (and fee-based) online courses. If you prefer to play around with some new tools, try a plug-in!

- To literally get your hands dirty in the world of architectural production, you can volunteer with organizations such as Habitat for Humanity or the Open Architecture Collaborative.

REFERENCES

Bergdoll, Barry, and Guy Nordenson, eds. *Rising Currents: Projects for New York's Waterfront*. New York, NY: Museum of Modern Art, 2011.

Borden, Iain, Murray Fraser, and Barbara Penner, eds. *Forty Ways to Think About Architecture: Architectural History and Theory Today*. Hoboken, NJ: John Wiley & Sons, 2014.

Brown, James Benedict, Harriet Harriss, Ruth Morrow, and James Soane, eds. *A Gendered Profession: The Question of Representation in Space Making*. Newcastle Upon Tyne, UK: RIBA Publishing, 2019.

Ching, Francis D. K. *Architecture: Form, Space, & Order*. Hoboken, NJ: John Wiley & Sons, 2007.

Ching, Francis D. K., Mark M. Jarzombek, and Vikramaditya Prakash. *A Global History of Architecture*. Hoboken, NJ: John Wiley & Sons, 2007.

Cole, Emily, ed. *The Grammar of Architecture*. Boston, MA: Bulfinch Press, 2002.

Elefante, Carl. "The Greenest Building Is . . . One That Is Already Built." *Journal of the National Trust for Historic Preservation* 21, no. 4 (2007): 26–38.

Fletcher, Margaret. *Constructing the Persuasive Portfolio: The Only Primer You'll Ever Need*. London, UK: Routledge, 2016.

Fraser, Murray, ed. *Design Research in Architecture: An Overview*. Surrey, UK: Ashgate Publishing Limited, 2013.

Frederick, Matthew. *101 Things I Learned in Architecture School*. Cambridge, MA: MIT Press, 2007.

Goode, Patrick, ed. *The Oxford Companion to Architecture*. Oxford, UK: Oxford University Press, 2009.

Holden, Robert, and Jamie Liversedge. *Landscape Architecture: An Introduction*. London, UK: Laurence King Publishing Ltd., 2014.

Ingersoll, Richard, and Spiro Kostof, eds. *World Architecture: A Cross-Cultural History*. 2nd ed. Oxford, UK: Oxford University Press, 2019.

Irving, Mark, ed. *1001 Buildings You Must See before You Die*. London, UK: Cassell Illustrated, 2007.

Mason, Randall, and Max Page, eds. *Giving Preservation a History: Histories of Historic Preservation in the United States*. 2nd ed. London, UK: Routledge, 2019.

Orff, Kate. *Toward an Urban Ecology: SCAPE*. New York, NY: The Monacelli Press, 2016.

Pevsner, Nikolaus. *An Outline of European Architecture*. Harmondsworth, UK: Penguin, 1943.

Robertson, Margaret. *Dictionary of Sustainability*. London, UK: Routledge, 2017.

_____. *Sustainability Principles and Practice*. 2nd ed. London, UK: Routledge, 2017.

Stein, Carl J. *Greening Modernism: Preservation, Sustainability, and the Modern Movement*. New York, NY: W. W. Norton, 2010.

Stratigakos, Despina. "Hollywood Architects." *Places Journal* (September 2016). doi:10.22269/160906.

Vitruvius, Pollio. *The Ten Books on Architecture*. Edited by Albert Andrew Howard, Morris Hicky Morgan, and Herbert Langford Warren. Translated by Morris Hicky Morgan. Cambridge, MA: Harvard University Press, 1914.

INDEX

ACKNOWLEDGMENTS

For more than a dozen years, I had the fortune to work with Duke University's Talent Identification Program, developing and implementing curriculum for students participating in on-site programs as well as online eStudies and independent learning. I also had the privilege of leading several design camps for middle- and high-school students while teaching at Auburn University (2014–2019). These endeavors have been invaluable to my conceptualization of and engagement with design education. I wholeheartedly believe that as architectural designers, historians, and stewards of the built environment, we need to do a better job of getting students involved with and excited about design at a young age.

Thank you to the interviewees who kindly offered their precious time and expertise and to the friends and colleagues who completed the Early Introductions to Design survey; your thoughts and reflections were invaluable. The team at Rockridge Press also facilitated the process of making this book a reality.

Thank you to my family members who enthusiastically welcome and encourage travel, curiosity, and chasing one's passion.

ABOUT THE AUTHOR

Dr. Danielle S. Willkens, Associate AIA, FRSA, LEED AP BD+C, is an assistant professor at the Georgia Institute of Technology's School of Architecture. She holds a B.S. in architecture and an M.Arch from the University of Virginia, an M.Phil in architectural history and theory from Cambridge University's St. John's College, a graduate certificate in historic preservation from Savannah College of Art & Design, and a Ph.D. in architectural history and theory from University College London's Bartlett School of Architecture. Her practice and research include design/build projects, public installations, and on-site investigations. She is an FAA-certified remote pilot. She was the 2015 recipient of the Society of Architectural Historians' H. Allen Brooks Travelling Fellowship, and her research has been supported by the Sir John Soane's Museum Foundation, the International Center for Jefferson Studies, and American Philosophical Society. Dedicated to expanding enrichment opportunities and pedagogical approaches in design education, she was awarded a 2017–2018 Association of Collegiate Schools of Architecture/American Institute of Architecture Students New Faculty Teaching Award.